MOTORCYCLES

pil

Publications International, Ltd.

Written by Doug Mitchel and Rick Cotta

Photography by Doug Mitchel

Additional photos courtesy of Ducati, Harley-Davidson, Honda, and the Library of Congress

Thanks to the owners of the motorcycles featured for their enthusiastic cooperation. They are listed below, along with the page number(s) on which their bikes appear:

Mike Abt, Countryside BMW, 142, 143; American Classics Museum, 84, 85; Jim Anderson, 80, 81; Larry Anderson, 76, 77; John Archacki, 84, 85; Tom Baer, 12, 13, 44, 45; Rex Barrett, 124, 125; Bob Baumgartner, 78, 79; Pete Bollenbach, 10, 11, 26, 27, 34, 35, 42, 43, 48, 49, 66, 67; Marvin Bredemeir, 74, 75; Don Chasteen, 90, 91; Vance Clute, 67; Dale Walksler's Wheels Through Time Museum, 24, 25, 52, 53, 62, 63, 70, 71, 84, 85; Tim Eiden, 108, 109; Henry Hardin Family, 20, 21, 22, 23, 60, 61; David Freeman, 136, 137, 140, 141; Harley-Davidson Motorcycle Company, 134, 135, 144; Heritage Harley-Davidson, 130, 131; Martin Horn, 102, 103; Illinois Harley-Davidson, 128, 129; Matt Jonas, 112, 113, 122, 123, 126, 127; Jim Kersting Family Collection, 38, 39, 50, 51, 60, 61, 98, 99, 120, 121; Dave Kiesow, Illinois Harley-Davidson, 54, 55; Ray Landy, 104, 105; Barbara Liles and Warren Dorn, 114, 115; Bob Maxant, Illinois Harley-Davidson, 30, 31; R. B. McClean, 18, 19, 88, 89; Kim, Jeff, and Kevin Minnis, 86, 87, 96; David Monahan, 70, 71; Ted Moran, 116, 117, 132, 133; John Murphy, 82, 83, 94, 95; John Olberg, 32, 33; Otis Chandler Museum, 14, 15, 16, 17, 28, 29, 36, 37, 40, 41, 56, 57, 58, 59; Leasha Overturf, 106, 107; Paul Ross, 46, 47; Steve Schifer, 92, 93; Robert Scott, 100, 101; Cloyd H. Spahr, 96, 97; Bob Stark, 62, 63; Al Steier, 110, 111; Jody Synove, 68, 69; Joe Tylus, 138, 139; Larry and Caroline West, 74, 75

Louis Weber, CEO
Publications International, Ltd.
8140 Lehigh Avenue
Morton Grove, IL 60053

ISBN: 978-1-68022-990-5

Manufactured in China.

8 7 6 5 4 3 2 1

Table of Contents

Foreword   **p. 004**

Chapter 1   **p. 006**
Inception to Military Utilization
1885–1945

Chapter 2   **p. 064**
Postwar European and Japanese Competition
1946–1978

Chapter 3   **p. 118**
Customization and Variation Run the Market
1979–2017

Foreword

Though most early motorcycles were essentially bicycles with small proprietary engines attached, the very first motorcycle, credited to Gottlieb Daimler and Paul Maybach of Germany, looked little like its successors. Built in 1885, it was a crude, wooden-framed contraption powered by a primitive gasoline engine and supported by a pair of training wheels, with the rider perched high on a thin leather saddle.

Like their automotive counterparts, numerous designs and powerplants were tried on early motorcycles. A few carried steam engines, though the weight and size of the necessary components quickly put this idea on the back burner. At least one mounted a radial engine inside the front wheel, which made for great traction and a simple driveline, but required the engine be stalled when coming to a stop. Even those that used conventional single-cylinder engines mounted them in different locations (sometimes over or beside the rear wheel), and fuel tank placement varied.

But by the early 1900s, most designs had reached a consensus: single-cylinder gasoline engine mounted between the frame downtubes with the fuel tank above it. Drive was typically by leather belt, with only one speed. Starting was accomplished by pedaling, either while on the center stand or going down the road. Thanks to the availability of proprietary engines from De Dion of France, Minerva of Belgium, and others, most early motorcycles were produced by backyard mechanics. As such, anyone with a bicycle to start with could become a "manufacturer," and there were literally hundreds in the early part of the 20th century.

However, competition weeded out most of these enterprises early on. As the surviving manufacturers tried to outdo one another, motorcycles became faster, more reliable, and more purpose-built, weaning themselves from their bicycle heritage. Engines gained more sophisticated intake and ignition systems, various forms of suspension were devised, drum brakes succeeded coaster brakes, transmissions and clutches were added, and kick levers replaced pedals for starting. Racing played a major role in these advancements, one of the oldest and most famous competitions being the Isle of Man Tourist Trophy race, held off the coast of England since 1907.

Then came World War I, which had a profound effect on motorcycling. The good news was that the war prompted engineering advances, but the bad news was that the wartime economy took its toll on several of the smaller makes. As a result, the state of technology advanced rapidly during the first decade of the 20th century, and machines built by the few survivors in the mid-1920s were surprisingly modern conveyances. Trouble was, a new and ominous foe was emerging.

Through the miracle of mass production, Henry Ford had been able to gradually decrease the cost of his Model T so that by 1925, prices were starting at less than $300—deep into motorcycle territory. Since it then became difficult to justify a motorcycle from a value standpoint, manufacturers began stressing the fun factor. Motorcycling became a "sport," and ads began touting the thrill and adventure of riding. This strategy seemed to work—right up until October 29, 1929.

The stock market crash had a devastating impact on all forms of business in the United States, and the motorcycle industry was no exception. Though the field had already narrowed considerably by that time, the Great Depression weeded out all the major American players save for Harley-Davidson and Indian. Those two companies managed to hang on through World War II, during which both supplied motorcycles to Allied forces. After hostilities ceased, European motorcycles were exported to the U.S. in ever-growing numbers, and these posed yet another challenge to the two remaining American manufacturers—one of whom wouldn't survive. Indian had been struggling since before the war, and was less able to face the onslaught of imports than was Harley-Davidson. It was a sad day when, in 1953, this venerable make finally closed its doors. U.S. importers tried slapping the name on a variety of smaller bikes over the years with little success, though a recent revival of a large American-built Indian V-twin seems to be gaining a foothold.

During the late 1940s and early 1950s, motorcycling received a black eye from groups of enthusiasts who tended to get... well... a little too enthusiastic. So when Japanese manufacturers began exporting small motorcycles to the United States later in the 1950s, they were pushed as being more "friendly." "You meet the nicest people on a Honda" proved to be a strong advertising campaign, opening the floodgates for Japanese imports. Yet despite this influx of competitors during the postwar period, few great strides were made from an engineering standpoint. But that was all about to change—and it would change virtually overnight.

More than 45 years later, it's difficult to describe the impact the Honda CB750 had on the marketplace when it was introduced for 1969. Though it carried little in the way of new features, it made its mark by combining state-of-the-art technology with Japanese reliability, all at a reasonable price. Yet its place in motorcycle history is assured not so much for what it *was,* as for what it *did.*

The overwhelming success of the Honda 750 prompted other Japanese manufacturers to engage in a furious battle of one-upmanship. Ever larger and faster models appeared with typical Japanese reliability and low prices, and this sounded the death knell for the comparatively stagnant British motorcycle industry—and nearly did in Harley-Davidson as well. But while the market was losing its British choices, it was gaining a wider variety of models. Scramblers, which were essentially street bikes mildly modified for off-pavement use, evolved into more specialized enduro and motocross machines. Cruisers offered custom styling right off the showroom floor. Long-distance riders found comfort in the new touring models, and high-performance sport bikes that mimicked fully faired racing machines became all the rage.

Virtually every industrialized nation has hosted a motorcycle manufacturer at one time or another, but only five countries produced machines that achieved international popularity: Germany, Great Britain, Italy, Japan, and the United States.

So that the evolution of the motorcycle can be easily observed, entries are arranged chronologically, starting with the crude conveyances of the early 1900s and running through today's sophisticated machines. Today's machines are far quicker, safer, more comfortable, and more reliable than those of years past, yet their riders still enjoy the freedom and adventure felt by those hardy souls who made early motorcycles their transportation of choice. *Motorcycles* celebrates some of the most memorable machines of the 20th and 21st centuries, and salutes the riders—both past and present—who have made this sport what it is today.

MOTOR

CYCLES

Chapter 1
Inception to Military Utilization
1885–1945

In their first 35 years of existence, motorcycles went from crazy experiment to common form of transportation. Much of their appeal was economic: They typically sold for a third the cost of the cheapest cars. By the early 1900s, numerous manufacturers had sprung up around the country. But few of these companies produced machines in any volume, and fewer still sold them nationally. These early motorcycles were quite primitive, but the state of the art advanced quickly once demand grew. Motors gained more sophisticated intake and ignition systems, various forms of suspension were devised, drum brakes succeeded coaster brakes, transmissions and clutches were added, and kick levers replaced pedals for starting. As technology advanced, so did sales—and so did competition.

By the 1920s, motorcycles had become a viable and accepted form of transportation. Yet due to World War I and the heat of competition, far fewer manufacturers remained in the game, the most prominent being Harley-Davidson, Indian, and Excelsior. The pace of technology slowed during the 1920s, but that isn't to say it stood still. Bicyclelike rear coaster brakes gave way to drum or external-band brakes, and front brakes—previously absent—started to appear. But the real focus during the 1920s was on styling. Fuel tanks became sleeker and more prominent, as did fenders. Tires and wheels were wider and meatier, while seats were lower to the ground. But none of this could compare to the changes that would result from the stock market crash of October 29, 1929, for the Great Depression that followed would have a profound effect on American business.

The Depression adversely affected all forms of business in the U.S., and the motorcycle industry was no exception. In fact, by 1932, only Harley-Davidson and Indian survived as major players. With cars getting cheaper, motorcycles became a hard sell based on price alone. So a new marketing approach was tried—that of selling motorcycling as a "sport" rather than merely a means of transportation. A greater emphasis was placed on styling, flashier paint jobs appeared, and more-powerful motors were introduced. And this—along with an improving economy—kept Harley-Davidson and Indian afloat during the lean years.

Just as the U.S. was recovering from the Depression, the country entered World War II. Civilian production of many items was curtailed so factories could turn to making war materiel. Harley-Davidson—and to a lesser extent, Indian—began building military-spec motorcycles, which brought in much-needed funds. And when civilian production resumed after the war, pent-up demand brought in even more.

1885 Daimler

Though most early motorcycles were essentially bicycles with small proprietary motors attached, the very first motorcycle looked little like its successors. Built in 1885 by Gottlieb Daimler and Paul Maybach of Germany, it was a crude, wooden-framed contraption powered by a primitive 264-cc gasoline motor developing about .5 horsepower. A pair of "training wheels" kept the machine upright, as the rider had to sit high atop the frame on a thin leather saddle. Top speed was 7 mph, about twice as fast as a normal walking pace.

1904 Indian

In the early 1900s, Oscar Hedstrom mounted a single-cylinder De Dion engine on a tandem bicycle for the purpose of pacing then-popular bicycle races. George Hendee, a bicycle manufacturer from Springfield, Massachusetts, saw the contraption at an event and proposed a cooperative effort to produce motorized bicycles commercially. Hedstrom agreed, and in 1901 the Indian Motorcycle Company was born.

Most pre-1910 motorcycles look as though the manufacturer simply bolted an engine and its accessories onto a common bicycle frame—which indeed was usually the case. But early Indians used the engine as a stressed frame member, effectively replacing the downtube beneath the seat. As with most motorcycles of the era, suspension was nonexistent (save for the spring-mounted seat), and pedals were used to start the engine. However, Indian used a direct-drive chain rather than the more common tensioned leather belt to turn the rear wheel, the chain being more positive in operation—and more reliable.

This 1904 "humpback" is little different than the first 1901 models. Producing just over two horsepower, the 13-cubic-inch single provided a top speed of around 25 mph. Both the lubrication and ignition system were of the "total loss" variety. Braking was accomplished by backpedaling, which activated a rear coaster brake.

Dark blue was the color of choice until 1904, when black and vermillion became optional. The vermillion would later be known as Indian Red.

1904 Marsh

The eastern coast of the U.S. was home to numerous motorcycle manufacturers in the industry's early days, and Marsh was one of the first. Located in Brockton, Massachusetts, the Marsh brothers built a motorized bicycle in 1899, with regular production commencing the following year. Unlike many early manufacturers, which used engines built by outside suppliers, Marsh made its own. Like most powerplants of the day, it had a single cylinder with an intake valve opened by suction created when the piston was on its downward stroke (called an "atmospheric intake valve") and a mechanically actuated side exhaust valve. The spark plug was fired by a "total loss" ignition system, meaning there was no generator to recharge the battery; when it went dead, it was recharged by an outside source or replaced.

Though the first production engines produced less than two horsepower, a racing engine offering six horsepower was built in 1902. The motorcycle it powered could reach nearly 60 mph, a blistering speed at the time. In 1905, the Marsh brothers teamed up with Charles Metz and the resulting motorcycles were called Marsh & Metz, or just M.M. The company was among the first to offer a V-twin, that being a 45-degree unit that arrived around 1906. Two years later, a 90-degree V-twin appeared, which was claimed to offer better internal balance. But the pioneering manufacturer didn't last long. Like many others of the era, M.M. folded under the weight of stiff competition, closing its doors in 1913.

1. Typical for motorcycles of the period, neither the front nor rear offered any kind of suspension system, though the leather saddle was mounted on springs.

2. Box beneath the seat carries the battery that powers the total loss ignition system; there is no generator. Chrome lever on side of fuel tank is the compression release, which cracks the exhaust valve open to ease starting.

3. Like most engines of the day, the 27-cubic-inch (442-cc) single had an atmospheric overhead intake valve and mechanically activated side exhaust valve. Also common was the use of the engine as a structural frame member.

1910 Pierce

While most motorcycles of the era were powered by singles or the occasional V-twin, Pierce topped them all with America's first four-cylinder machine. Unfortunately, the design—and the company—would be short-lived.

Introduced in 1909, Pierce's four-cylinder model was influenced by the FN four built in Belgium. The low-slung Pierce, however, looked far more modern than the FN, and was a high quality bike built around a heavy tubular frame that doubled as the fuel and oil tanks. Power came from a "T-head" engine displacing 700 ccs—about 42 cubic inches. It was a stressed part of the frame and drove the rear wheel through an enclosed shaft, another American first.

Pierce's four was a stately machine that was expensive to buy and even more expensive to build. The 700-cc "Flathead" four was of "T-head" configuration, with the intake and exhaust valves on opposite sides of the cylinder. This resulted in a "crossflow" design that was theoretically more efficient than a conventional "side valve" engine with the two valves sitting next to each other. Fuel was carried in the top and rear frame tubes, oil in the front tube. Front suspension was a conventional leading link, but with an enclosed spring. Shaft drive was a first for American-made bikes.

Early models were direct drive, with no clutch and no gearbox; in 1910, a clutch and two-speed transmission were added. Pierce's four was an expensive machine that saw limited sales. Though a less-expensive single cylinder model of similar design was offered as well, both were rumored to cost more than their retail prices to build, and financial shortfalls forced the company to close its doors in 1913.

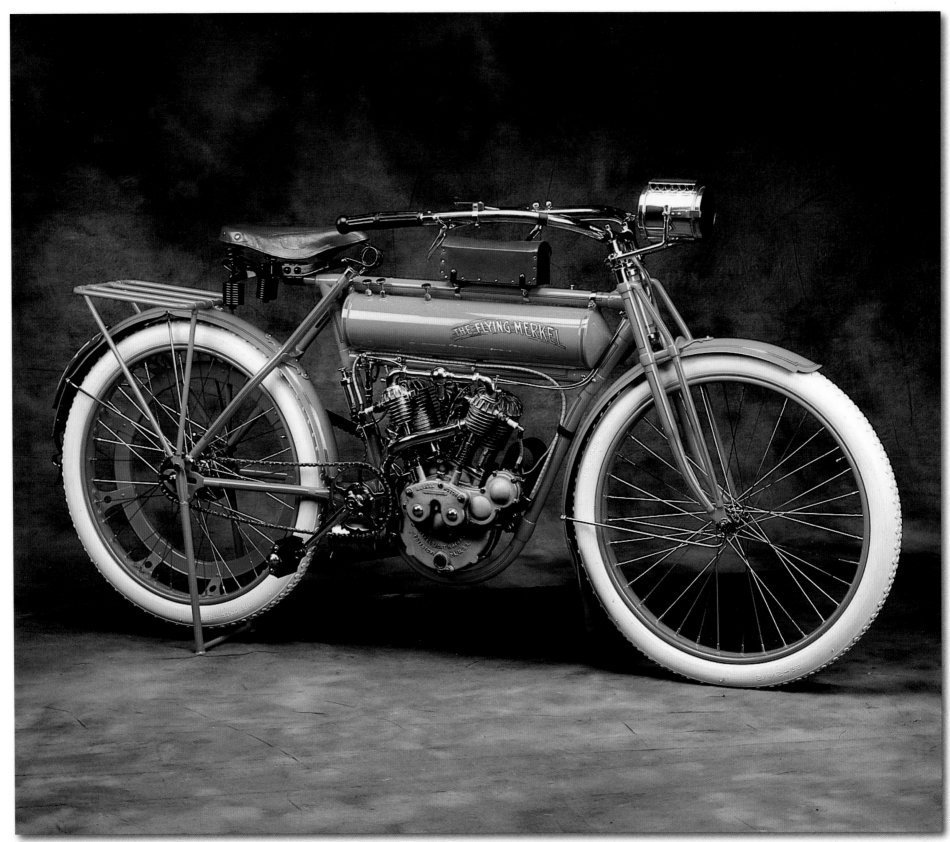

1911 Flying Merkel

In the early days of motorcycling, Merkels were the bikes to beat. Small singles of 1902 evolved into thundering V-twins by 1910, at which point the machines adopted the aptly descriptive "Flying Merkel" moniker.

The company was also known for innovation. Front forks that looked rigid were actually mounted on sliders with enclosed springs either at the top of the sliders or inside the frame neck. The design that became known as "Merkel-style" forks were popular add-ons to other manufacturers' racing bikes. Merkel also was a pioneer in rear suspension; 1910 models offered modern swingarm designs incorporating sliders similar to those used on the forks.

None of this, however, was enough to keep the Flying Merkel aloft. Despite 1915 models that offered a kick-starter, front and rear suspension, sprung saddle, two-speed planetary transmission, and a powerful 1000-cc intake-over-exhaust V-twin, they would prove to be the final offerings of one of motorcycling's most innovative pioneers.

①

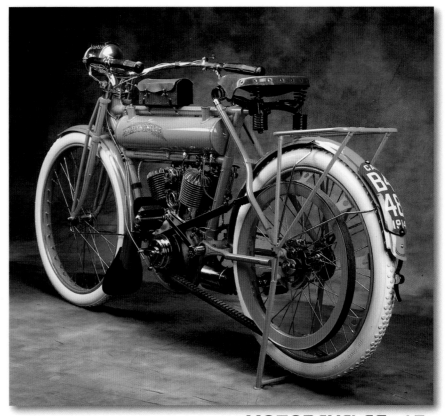

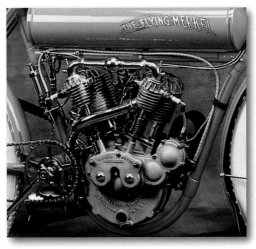

1. Flying Merkels of 1911 offered V-twins of 885 and 1000 ccs, along with the customary single-speed belt drive. But these bikes were far ahead of their time in the suspension department, offering simple but effective "Merkel-style" forks in front, and a swingarm suspension in back.

1911 Excelsior

Mr. Ignatz Schwinn had been in the business of building bicycles for several years when he decided to capitalize on the motorcycling craze that was sweeping the nation. By combining a 500-cc De Dion single-cylinder engine with a stout bicycle frame, Schwinn put the first Excelsior motorcycle on sale in 1908—or at least, the first Excelsior motorcycle to be built in the United States. Strangely, the name was already in use on motorcycles produced by separate companies in both Germany and England.

Although it produced some small two-strokes, Excelsior was better known for its four-stroke singles and V-twins, the latter arriving in 1910. All of the four-stroke models used "F-head" (overhead intake, side exhaust) engines of Excelsior's own design. For 1911, the 30-cubic-inch single could be ordered with a choice of magneto or battery electrical system. The leading-link front fork provided only a small amount of travel, but that was more than was afforded by the rigid frame in back. As was common for the era, the single was driven by a wide leather belt, with progress slowed by a rear coaster brake.

1. Before the advent of modern cables, control motions were transferred by intricate jointed shafts.

2. Note the fancy "engine-turned" finish on the crankcase. The Excelsior's rear frame tube took a detour in order to clear the large drive pulley.

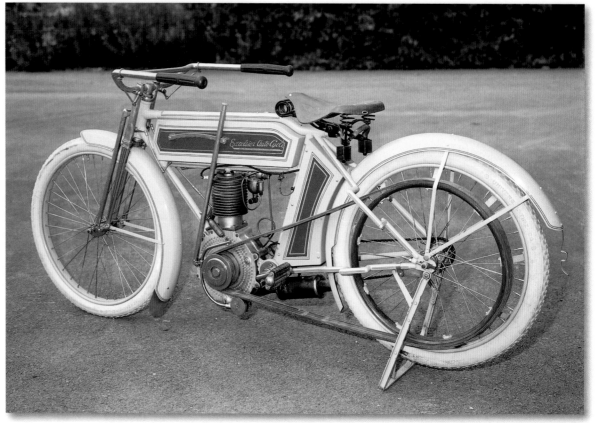

1912 Harley-Davidson X8A

Harley-Davidson's first motorcycle, little more than a bicycle with a single-cylinder three-horsepower engine mounted within the frame tubes, was built in 1903. Though the V-twins that would make the company famous appeared six years later, single-cylinder machines continued to represent the bulk of Harley's sales. By 1912, public demand for more power was answered with the X8A, which was powered by a 30-cubic inch single producing 4.3 horsepower.

A hand-operated oil pump was added to augment the existing gravity-feed system, and a magneto ignition was used for easier starting. Also new this year was the "Free Wheel Control," one of the industry's first clutch systems. With it, smooth takeoffs from a standing start were possible for the first time.

The issue of comfort was also addressed. Joining Harley's traditional leading-link front fork was the new "Full Floating" saddle, in which a coil spring mounted inside the vertical frame tube cushioned the seat post, while the rear of the seat was supported by two more coils. Though this was hardly a substitute for a real rear suspension, it was as good as Harley riders would get for another 45 years.

1. Tall lever on left side of tank activated the "Free Wheel Control," Harley's early clutch system. While many companies had gone to a mechanical intake valve by this time, the X8A stuck with an atmospheric intake valve, located beneath the small dome at the top of the engine's right side.

1913 Excelsior 7-C

Excelsior was once a big name in motorcycling, often ranking just behind Indian and Harley-Davidson in popularity. Since the company's inception in 1907 as a division of the larger Schwinn Bicycle concern, its motorcycles were in a constant state of improvement, as there was plenty of research and development talent on tap.

In 1910, the company's single-cylinder motorcycle was joined by an 800-cc V-twin. The V-twin soon grew to 1000 ccs and replaced the drive belt with a chain in 1913. By this time, the old leading-link forks had been supplanted by a trailing-link arrangement activating a leaf spring, but despite the added speed potential, the Excelsior still relied on a simple rear coaster brake. Soon afterward, a three-speed transmission was adopted, replacing the former single-speed unit.

The next advancement was the "Big Valve Motor" using large 2⅛-inch valves, which brought the company a fair degree of racing success. With it, Excelsior officially broke the 100-mph barrier on a wooden track in 1912.

Since his interest in the world of motorcycles was growing, Ignatz Schwinn purchased the financially troubled Henderson Company in 1917 and expanded his line to include Henderson's inline-four model. This new acquisition pushed the Excelsiors into the shadows as the big Henderson grew in popularity.

But just as quickly as the inspiration had come, Ignatz Schwinn seemed to lose interest in motorcycling. By 1931, both Henderson and Excelsior had joined the growing number of marques that had blossomed during motorcycling's boom years only to succumb to stiff competition and a depressed economy in the early 1930s.

1913 Indian 61 Twin

Indian offered its first V-twin in 1907, a 40-cubic-inch (633-cc) unit with atmospheric intake valves, common at the time. By 1913, it had grown to 61 cubic inches and boasted overhead intake and side exhaust valves. Though standard models had but a single speed, a two-speed transmission was available as an option.

Indian built singles during this period as well, but the V-twin accounted for 90 percent of the company's production. It's not difficult to see why: In 1913, for example, a four-horsepower single cost $200, while a seven-horsepower twin went for $250—quite a performance bargain.

New for 1913 was a "Cradle Spring Frame" that incorporated the world's first swingarm rear suspension system—though it was somewhat different in design than what we commonly see today. When the rear wheel encountered a bump, two vertical rods actuated a pair of leaf springs attached to the frame beneath the seat. This joined a conventional (at least for Indian) trailing-link front fork that worked in a similar fashion. For those suspicious of the new technology, a rigid frame remained available. Braking was accomplished with an internal-shoe/external-band rear brake, which incidentally conformed to Britain's "dual brake" requirement for motorcycles sold in that country—though it might not have been exactly what the Brits had in mind.

1. Indian's swingarm rear suspension, which appeared in 1913, was an industry first. It joined a front suspension of similar design, both incorporating leaf springs.

2. Further comforting the rider was a sprung saddle using—you guessed it—leaf springs. The upright cylindrical plunger beneath the seat is a small oil pump that allows the rider to feed more oil to the engine during periods of hard use or when traveling uphill.

1914 Sears Deluxe

In the early catalogs from Sears and Roebuck, you could order almost anything—including a house. But it was in the 1912 catalog that Sears offered its first motorcycle. This 1914 magneto model, complete with the 35-cubic-inch Deluxe "Big Five" engine, sold for $197.50 and was claimed to have nearly the same power as the larger twin-cylinder models.

These single-cylinder versions were available with either batteries or a Bosch magneto. Two twin-cylinder motorcycles were offered, one producing seven horsepower, the other nine. The engines in all Sears machines were manufactured by Spake, which sold them to a variety of builders.

As with most makers of motorcycles in this period, Sears claimed high quality and proven performance for its models. The handlebars were made of double reinforced tubing and the fuel tank was formed out of anti-rust material. A trailing-link fork with leaf-spring handled suspension chores in front, but a seat mounted on coil springs had to make do in the rear.

Sears only sold these early motorcycles until 1916, when they were removed from the catalog. But between 1953 and 1963, Sears offered a line of cycles manufactured by Puch under the Sears-Allstate moniker.

1. Tank-mounted speedometer is driven off a spiral gear on the rear hub. Sears used a trailing-link leaf-spring front suspension similar to Indian's.

2. Bosch magneto sits ahead of the finely machined crankcase of the 35-cubic-inch Spake-built single. Lever beside the engine controls the clutch; pedal at lever's base activates the two-speed rear hub.

1914 Thor

Thor played an instrumental role in the early years of motorcycle history, not for its machines as much as its engines. Many early manufacturers got their start mounting Thor powerplants in frames of their own choosing.

Owned by the Aurora Automatic Machinery Company, Thor began building engines for Indian in 1902. Later clients of note included Reading Standard and Sears, along with a host of lesser-known makes. When the contract with Indian ran out in 1907, Thor began building its own motorcycles. Early examples used a version of the Indian-designed single Thor had been producing for five years, and when Thor introduced its first V-twin in 1910, it was essentially the same engine with another cylinder bolted to the cases. But unlike most such designs, it was tilted forward so that the rear cylinder stood straight up, leaving room behind for the magneto and carburetor.

By 1913, Thor had introduced a new V-twin of its own design, and this one was mounted in the conventional manner. Displacing 76 cubic inches, it enjoyed some racing success, but was always in the shadows of Indian and Harley-Davidson on the track.

Like so many other manufacturers of the period, Thor eventually succumbed to a competitive environment. Its last motorcycles were built in 1917, after which the parent company concentrated on power tools and appliances.

1. The V-twin was of conventional intake-over-exhaust layout, but Thor ran the intake pushrods between the cylinder fins, where most manufacturers mounted them externally.

2. Single- and two-speed drive were offered, the latter shown here with its crankshaft-mounted transmission.

1915 Harley-Davidson 11F

Technology advanced rapidly at Harley-Davidson during the 1909–1915 time frame. The company's first V-twin arrived in 1909, though it was taken off the market in 1910 to fix some bugs and reintroduced the next year. This was followed by chain drive and one of the industry's first clutches in 1912, and a two-speed rear hub in 1914, which also saw the advent of floorboards and the step starter. For 1915, a proper three-speed transmission was offered, along with a magneto and electric lighting system incorporating a taillight that could be removed for use as a nighttime service light. The model shown, however, is equipped with a Prest-O-Lite headlight, which is powered by acetylene gas.

Harley-Davidson's 61-cubic-inch "F-head" V-twin, while not a true overhead-valve design (only the intake was OHV), was more advanced than the "Flathead" engines that powered some competitors. Furthermore, the 1915 models gained an automatic oiler and larger intake valves, the latter helping to boost output to 11 horsepower. That rating, by the way, was guaranteed by Harley-Davidson, the only motorcycle manufacturer to back its quoted power claims in writing.

Elsewhere, the 11F was perhaps not so advanced. The expanding-band rear brake now featured double action to increase braking efficiency, yet was far from state of the art, and the front suspension remained a leading-link arrangement with coil springs that allowed only slightly more wheel travel than the nonexistent rear suspension.

1. Electric lighting was newly available this year, but many riders had more faith in the old acetylene system.

2. An exposed valve train was common in the era, and must have been fascinating—and messy in action.

3. View from the driver's seat, looking down at the fuel tank, which also carried oil. Shifter had a gated guide plate.

4. Barely able to reach the handlebars, this little tyke is no doubt dreaming of the day he can ride a motorcycle of his own.

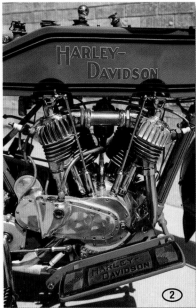

1916 Harley-Davidson J

From a styling standpoint, the 1916 Harley-Davidsons were a great leap forward. Fuel tanks now had rounded rather than square-cut corners, and the whole bike took on a longer, lower appearance. Also, pedals no longer sprouted from the lower frame on models with the three-speed transmission, which now sported a modern kick-starter.

Other than the kick-starter, however, there were few mechanical changes of note. Forks remained a leading-link design with enclosed coil springs, and the 61-cubic-inch intake-over-exhaust V-twin received only a curved intake manifold to smooth the airflow into the cylinders.

This would be the last year Harleys would wear their traditional grey paint, which had graced the machines since 1906. Its replacement—Olive Drab—would be hardly more colorful, yet would enjoy an equally long tenure.

1. Among the few mechanical changes was a curved intake manifold to feed the venerable "F-head" V-twin.

2. This model J is fitted with the optional electric lighting that had become available in 1915.

3. The magneto, located behind the engine, was switched on and off with a key—no doubt an effort to deter would-be "borrowers."

4. Fitted with a sidecar and passenger seat (affixed to the luggage rack behind the dapper lad), motorcycles of the era often served as family transportation.

1918 Pope L-18

Pope Manufacturing Company had been building Pope-Tribune automobiles and Columbia bicycles for years before they combined the two concepts and began producing motorcycles in 1911. Those early models were singles, but a V-twin followed in 1912, and by 1918, Pope was known for quality construction and innovative engineering.

This 61-cubic-inch V-twin illustrates the point well. It features overhead valves at a time when most competitors offered "Flathead" or "F-head" engines. Crankcases were cast from an aluminum alloy, and each set of pistons and connecting rods were matched with another pair of the exact weight. Its armored magneto ignition allowed use in all types of weather. The front suspension consisted of a trailing link actuating a leaf spring. But perhaps the most intriguing aspect of this Pope is the rear suspension. Not only was having any rear suspension unusual at that time, but the design was uniquely Pope. Unlike the common swingarm that is used on motorcycles today, Pope mounted the rear axle in a carrier that moved up and down between two posts, compressing a pair of springs on impact. Wheel travel was minimal, but something was better than nothing, and this became a major selling feature.

Unfortunately, this 1918 Pope represents the last of the line. With World War I raging in Europe, Pope suspended motorcycle production later that year to concentrate on building machine guns, and after the war, only the bicycle portion of the business was revived.

1920 Ace

Brothers Tom and William Henderson began building their famous four-cylinder motorcycles in 1912, but after running into financial trouble, sold out in 1918 to Excelsior, the motorcycle arm of the Schwinn Bicycle Company. Yet within two years, William formed Ace to produce a similar four-cylinder motorcycle, though no parts were interchangeable with the Hendersons.

Ace produced a great product, but proved to be a short-lived proposition. The firm was suffering financial setbacks when William was killed in a motorcycle accident in 1922, and production ceased two years later. Indian Motorcycle Company purchased Ace in 1927, and continued to offer what was essentially the Ace four—wearing Indian logos, of course—until World War II.

The Ace was powered by an "F-head" inline four displacing 77 cubic inches. Power was transferred through a foot-operated multidisc wet clutch to a three-speed transmission with hand shift. The leading-link front fork compressed a cartridge-type internal-coil spring, but the rear wheel was attached to a rigid frame.

Weighing in at about 395 lb, the Ace wasn't particularly light, but proved to be both powerful and durable. Several transcontinental records were set on virtually stock machines, and a "hopped up" version called the XP4 set a record speed of 129 mph in 1923. The fact that this motorcycle continued in production for over two decades with little more than suspension and brake updates is further testament to its endearing design.

1. Cartridge-type internal-coil spring gave a cleaner front-end appearance than did the exposed front springs of most competitors.

2. Ace's "F-head" inline four displaced 77 cubic inches, making it larger than most V-twins of the era.

3. Like many bikes of the day, Ace used an external-contracting rear brake, where the friction band gripped the outside of a metal drum.

1925 Harley-Davidson JD

With the JD model of 1925, Harley-Davidson made great strides in modernizing its machines—at least from the standpoint of styling. A new frame placed the saddle three inches lower than before, wider but smaller-diameter tires gave the bike a huskier look, and the fuel tank took on a rounded teardrop shape. Color choices, however, remained the same as they had since 1917: anything the customer wanted, as long as they wanted Olive Drab.

Since Harleys still lacked rear suspension, riders appreciated the softer fork springs and new contoured saddle, the latter of which also offered six-position height adjustment. The shift lever was moved farther forward along the side of the tank for convenience, and a fork-mounted tool kit made a debut appearance. Sidecars were popular accessories of the day, as these vehicles often served as a family's primary form of motorized transportation.

The first of Harley's famed 74-cubic-inch V-twins was introduced in 1922 and continued with only minor changes through 1928. Some of those minor changes occurred in the JD: Iron alloy pistons replaced the previous aluminum slugs, and 16 Alemite fittings were added to the engine and gearbox to ease lubrication.

1926 Cleveland

Cleveland bought into the motorcycle business in 1902 by slapping its name on a generic machine built by American Cycle Manufacturing Company. It was not alone. Columbia, Tribune, Rambler, and a host of others got started the same way—with essentially the same motorcycle. Aside from mounting the motor in a separate cradle between the diamond frame and rear wheel, these bikes were all very similar to Indians of the period.

Later Clevelands were more distinctive. Frames were long, low, and oddly configured, since they held a small two-stroke single that was mounted transversely with its crankshaft parallel to the bike's centerline. The two-speed transmission turned the power 90 degrees to culminate in chain drive to the rear wheel. Simple, light, and inexpensive, this model met with a fair degree of commercial success. But the market yearned for four-strokes, and Cleveland obliged.

After a brief run of four-stroke singles, Cleveland pulled out all the stops and introduced a four-cylinder model in 1926. Its 600-cc "T-head" engine ("Flathead" with intake valve on one side of the cylinder, exhaust on the other) was much smaller than most fours, and even many V-twins. Like the singles that preceded it, the crankshaft ran along the bike's centerline, but the transmission (now a three speed) turned the power to allow for a chain-driven rear wheel—same as Ace, Henderson, and Indian fours, though some others used a shaft. Because of its small displacement, Cleveland's four was not an impressive performer, so it was quickly followed by a conventional "Flathead" version that grew to 750 ccs and then 1000 ccs. Though the last, introduced in 1927, was the first production motorcycle with a front brake, its high price proved an insurmountable detriment when the Great Depression hit, and production ceased shortly thereafter.

1. Left-side shot reveals the shift lever, cast floorboard, updraft carburetor, rear-brake pedal, and behind the kick-starter, the generator, which was belt-driven off the magneto.

2. At 600 ccs, Cleveland's four was smaller than most others, and performance wasn't up to the market's demands. Clutch pedal actuated an automotive-style clutch.

3. Mounted just ahead of the fuel tank, oil-pressure and ammeter gauges were evidently considered more important than a speedometer—though the Cleveland wasn't that slow.

1926 Indian Prince

Indian's fortunes rose and fell during the Roaring Twenties, but in 1926 when this Prince was built, the company was on a high. Intended as an entry-level vehicle, the Prince was promoted on the slogan "You can learn to ride it in five minutes." Of course, Indian hoped those lured into motorcycling by the amiable Prince would return to buy a larger, more expensive Chief, or perhaps the soon-to-be-released inline-four model.

With its 21-cubic-inch "Flathead" single and manageable 265-lb curb weight, the Prince made an ideal first motorcycle. Like most others of the period, it had a spring-mounted seat to make up for the lack of rear suspension. In front, girder-style forks compressed a coil spring to provide a nominal amount of suspension travel. Also common for the era was the three-speed transmission and single drum brake fitted to the rear wheel.

A number of improvements marked the 1926 edition of the Prince. Most noticeable was the European-inspired rounded fuel tank that replaced the wedge-shaped tank used earlier. A redesigned saddle lowered the seat height a few inches, and handlebars were lengthened to reduce the long reach to the grips.

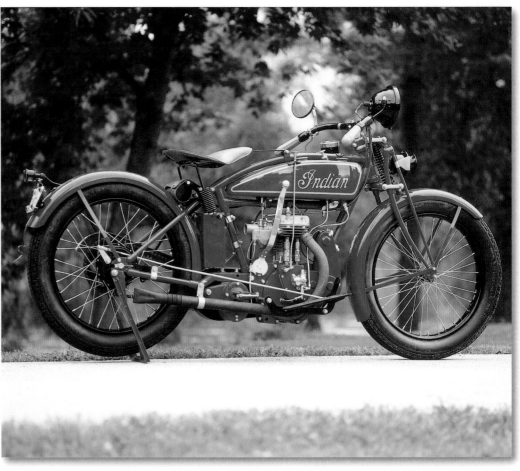

1927 Harley-Davidson BA

Though economical to buy and run, Harley's 21-cubic-inch single never sold particularly well during its ten-year production run. However, competition versions, known as "peashooters" due to the sound of their exhaust note, claimed many victories at the hands of Joe Petrali during the same period.

Two versions of the single were offered: a "Flathead" with eight horsepower and an overhead-valve variant producing twelve horsepower—an impressive 50 percent increase. Yet the "Flathead" sold better due to its lower cost and easier maintenance. Both could be fitted with electric lighting like the "Flathead" shown.

America's preference for big, powerful twins led to the demise of these single-cylinder models in the 1930s. Harley continued for a time with a larger 30.5-cubic-inch single and made several later attempts at selling single-cylinder machines, but it was always V-twins for which the company was best known.

1934 Harley-Davidson VLD

Harley's traditional Olive Drab paint—which had been used with little variation since 1917—was dropped as the standard color after 1932, to be replaced by more vibrant two-tones such as the black and Orlando Orange of our featured machine. Olive Drab, however, remained available for traditionalists.

"Flathead" V-twins, which had replaced "F-head" versions in the 1920s, came in 45- and "Big Twin" 74-cubic-inch versions. These were landmark engines; the 45 would continue to power three-wheeled Servi-Cars into the 1970s, and the Big Twin would form the basis for the famous EL overhead-valve "Knucklehead" of 1936.

Triggered by a stock-market crash on October 29, 1929, the Great Depression killed off all the major U.S. motorcycle manufacturers save for Harley-Davidson and Indian—and despite decreased competition, even those makes teetered on the brink of extinction. But Harley had a strong dealer network and the right products at the right time, and things were beginning to look up by 1934.

Harley's two-place Buddy Seat with sprung seat post arrived in 1933, quickly becoming one of the company's most popular accessories. Previously, passengers rode on a separate seat, usually mounted to the luggage rack.

1. Despite the introduction of the more modern overhead-valve "Knucklehead" Big Twin in 1936, the "Flathead" version would live on into the late 1940s.

2. The sweep of the rear fender is accented by artful two-toning. Note the hinge above the taillight; the rear part of the fender swings up to allow for tire changes.

3. Horn is embossed with Harley's bar-and-shield logo.

4. With her sailing cap at a jaunty tilt, this young lady looks ready to ride.

5. In 1917, Harley-Davidson adopted military Olive Drab as its standard—and only—color. Initially done in support of U.S. troops in World War I, it became a tradition that was maintained for a decade after the war was over.

1935 Indian Chief

With the 1927 debut of the Ace-based four-cylinder model, the V-twin Chief was demoted to second fiddle in Indian's line. Yet the 74-cubic-inch Chief, which competed directly with the large Harley-Davidsons of the time, continued as the company's top seller.

The big Chief was anything but graceful in slow-paced maneuvers, its suspension design, long wheelbase, and curb weight of 480 lb conspired to make it feel clumsy around town. Once up to speed, however, these same features provided exceptional stability.

Buyers of a 1935 Chief were faced with a wide variety of options. Color choices were reduced that year to 13, though an extra $5.00 would buy any hue DuPont offered. Even the fuel and oil tanks were available in three different trim variations. An optional "Y" engine featured aluminum cylinder heads, heavy-duty valve springs, and a modified muffler. A four-speed transmission could be ordered to replace the standard three speed. New to the 1935 version were redesigned fenders with larger valances to smooth out the styling, and a rebound spring for the ungainly front leaf suspension that helped smooth out the ride somewhat. Chiefs still lacked any form of rear suspension, though they did offer a spring-loaded seat post.

1936 DKW SB 500 A

German-based DKW began building motorcycles in 1919, starting with a one-horsepower engine in a bicycle frame. By the 1920s, the company had grown to become one of the largest producers of motorcycles in the world. Not only did DKW build its own machines, it also supplied two-stroke engines to other manufacturers, and even built automobiles from 1929 until the late 1960s.

Before the outbreak of World War II, DKW had amassed an impressive racing record, including a win at the Isle of Man TT event in 1938. During the war, DKWs saw extensive use on battlefields throughout Europe.

The 494-cc (30-cubic-inch) twin in the SB 500 A resulted from combining two separate 247-cc cylinders on a single block. Fed by a Bing carburetor, the two-stroke engine produced 15 horsepower. As did many bikes of the period, the DKW had a three-speed transmission with a hand shifter and foot-operated clutch. Also common for the era were the girder front fork and rigid rear frame.

"A" models differed from regular SB 500s in that they had a stronger frame fitted with a larger fuel tank and twin headlights. They also had electric start, a rare feature for that time; by contrast, Harley-Davidson didn't offer an electric starter until 1965.

1936 Harley-Davidson EL

Compared with the rampant speculation that preceded it, the official introduction of the 1936 EL was a bit anticlimactic. Dealers got the facts at their annual convention in December 1935, and, although not as wild as the rumors had predicted, the 61-cubic-inch EL nevertheless set new standards for Harley-Davidson—not to mention the rest of the industry.

Most important was the V-twin's switch from a "Flathead" design to overhead valves. Due to the resulting shape of the new rocker covers, the engine was dubbed "Knucklehead" by owners, a nickname by which it is still fondly known today. Equally significant was the new recirculating oiling system that eliminated the messiness and inconvenience of the previous "total loss" setup.

Unique to the 1936 EL are the rocker-shaft covers and air intake. The timing case cover was changed three times during the model year, each design a bit smoother than the last. Fuel tanks were welded and much sleeker than earlier examples, and the tank-mounted instrument cluster started a styling trend that continues to this day.

Despite the efficiency advantages of the EL's overhead-valve arrangement, Harley-Davidson continued to sell "Flathead" V-twin motorcycles for many years to come. But the EL would go on to become one of the most popular Harley-Davidson models of all time, and its overhead-valve engine established a configuration that has been used for all the company's V-twins ever since.

1. Harley-Davidsons have always been popular with police departments; this restored EL was originally put into service by the California Highway Patrol.

2. This "Christmas" edition EL displays one of the many color combinations available on Harleys of the era.

3. "Knucklehead" nickname came from the engine's rocker-cover caps, which were originally round and held in with a screw, but were soon replaced by large hex-head bolts.

4. Like most motorcycles of the day, Harleys used a hand shift/foot clutch arrangement; with shift lever all the way forward and "heel" down on the clutch pedal, the bike is shown in first gear with clutch disengaged.

5. The tank-mounted instrument panel, still a Harley styling element, included amp and oil-pressure readouts.

6. "Fishtail" muffler was another period styling touch, but was hard to see in basic black. Note frame-mounted toolbox with Harley decal.

1938 Harley-Davidson UL

After recovering from a difficult period in the early 1930s, Harley-Davidson was poised to forge ahead with a complete lineup that included 11 different models. It was built around Big Twin engines of 61, 74, or 80 cubic inches, all of which shared several components. However, the 61-cubic-inch V-twin was the famous "Knucklehead" with overhead valves, while the 74- and 80-cubic-inch V-twins had side valves.

The UL was a Sport Solo model with a 74-cubic inch "Flathead" powerplant. "Flatheads" had been modernized in 1937 with the adoption of the recirculating oiling system introduced on the "Knucklehead" the year before, and in 1938 gained more subtle changes: Higher handlebars resulted in a more comfortable riding position, the instrument panel was simplified by replacing the ammeter with a red warning lamp and the oil-pressure gauge with a green lamp, and new colors and striping were made available.

Surprisingly, Big Twin "Flatheads" remained in the Harley line for a dozen years after the debut of the famed "Knucklehead" overhead-valve models. And the smaller 45-cubic-inch "Flathead" V-twin continued to power three-wheeled Servi-Cars into the 1970s—both indications that many riders continued to admire the inherent simplicity of the "Flathead" design.

1938 Brough Superior SS 100

As the son of an early English motorcycle manufacturer, George Brough branched out on his own after World War I to build what would later be described as "the Rolls-Royce of motorcycles." These were expensive, well-finished machines compiled largely from proprietary components, most notably a 60 cubic-inch J.A.P. V-twin engine.

An early example was called the SS 80, so-named for its guaranteed top speed of 80 mph. Switching from "Flathead" to overhead-valve engines brought the SS 100 in 1924. Though smaller V-twins and even a four-cylinder sidecar model with an Austin automotive drivetrain were offered, the company's legacy lies with its big V-twins.

The exemplary engineering and construction for which Brough Superiors were famous can be seen in our featured example's leading-link front suspension with driver-adjustable damping, nickel-plated side panels on the fuel tank, foot-operated gearshift, contoured saddlebags, and plunger rear suspension. Though renowned primarily for their fine craftsmanship, Brough Superiors also held many speed records during the 1920s and 1930s, culminating in a 1937 run of nearly 170 mph on—of course—a modified version.

In the annals of motorcycle history, Brough Superior will always be aligned with famed military figure and writer T. E. Lawrence—Lawrence of Arabia. Being a personal friend of George Brough, Lawrence owned several Brough Superiors, and sadly, died on one.

1. Leading-link forks carried a separate rod tied to a driver-adjustable leather-faced damper.

2. Even the gas caps exuded quality.

3. Smith's speedometer advanced in chronograph-like clicks.

1940 Crocker

In a discussion of post-Depression American V-twins, Harley-Davidson and Indian are undoubtedly the best-known makes. But in terms of performance, neither could hold a candle to a Crocker. While the original Crockers were single-cylinder speedway machines, the first production models were large-displacement V-twins. Manufactured in Los Angeles, California, from 1936 to 1940, only 61 Crocker V-twins were built, making the survivors very rare indeed.

Contrary to some rumors, the Crocker used no Indian or Harley-Davidson components. Albert Crocker had enough experience to design and produce most of the parts at the company's Los Angeles location. Since Crockers were built to special order, displacement was up to the customer; some engines were as large as 100 cubic inches.

However, all Crocker production V-twins had overhead valves; early models had a hemispherical head with exposed valve springs, while later models had a flat, squish-type combustion chamber with enclosed valve springs. Most were magneto-fired, with carburetors by Linkert or Schebler. All came with a nearly indestructible three-speed transmission, the housing for which was cast into the frame.

Two different V-twins were offered: a Big Tank model and a Small Tank version, both fuel tanks being made of cast aluminum. The latter could be easily identified by the two mounting bolts that ran all the way through the tank halves. It also had a more upright fork angle that shortened the wheelbase and quickened the steering, making it better suited to racing.

On the street, at least, Crockers were formidable machines, able to humble most other bikes of the era. But due to their small numbers, few riders ever saw one—which is just as well, considering the humiliation that could follow.

1942 Harley-Davidson WLA & XA

WLA

Though rival Indian also supplied motorcycles to the U.S. military during World War II, the majority of those used in battle were Harley-Davidson WLAs. Wearing the requisite Olive Drab paint, these were 45-cubic-inch V-twins fitted with special equipment for wartime use. Items such as an ammo box, machine-gun scabbard, and rear carrier are obvious; less so are the special "blackout lights" front and rear that projected only a small sliver of light in an effort to avoid detection. In all, roughly 80,000 WLAs were built, many being sold as surplus after the war. These were often stripped down and fitted with aftermarket parts, fueling the rapidly developing customizing trend.

XA

Rare when new—and even more so today—was the Harley XA that was intended for desert use. In a vast departure for Harley-Davidson, the engine was a horizontally opposed twin—similar to BMWs of the day—and it drove the rear wheel through a foot-shift transmission with hand clutch (production Harleys of the day were all hand shift/foot clutch) and a jointed shaft instead of a chain. A girder-style fork handled suspension chores in front, while at the rear was a "plunger" suspension as used on contemporary Indians. However, only 1,000 XAs were built, and none saw service overseas.

1. Harley's XA, with its horizontally opposed twin and shaft drive, was designed for desert warfare, but never was used in combat.

2. The small blackout light on the front fender was used when concealment was necessary; a similar taillight is found at the rear.

3. A metal plate engraved with pertinent maintenance data was mounted on top of the fuel tank for quick reference.

4. Note the shock absorber added to the front suspension.

1. *"Model 841"*

2. Like their Harley counterparts, Indian's military bikes were sold as surplus after the war, as were spare engine/transmission combinations—the latter a do-it-yourselfer's dream at just $127.50.

1942 Indian 741 & 841

741

Like Harley-Davidson, Indian built military models of conventional V-twin design and shaft-drive "desert" configuration for use in World War II.

Indian's primary machine, the 741, carried a 30.5-cubic-inch "Flathead" V-twin based on the civilian 3050 model. Less powerful than Harley's 45-cubic-inch WLA, the 741 was used mainly by couriers and scouts, as what it lacked in performance it made up for in durability. A hand-shifted three-speed transmission and foot-operated clutch were fitted, both being normal practice for the day. It must have been confusing for a serviceman to go from an Indian to a Harley, however, because the Indian's clutch was engaged when the lever was pushed down with the heel, while a Harley's engaged by pushing down with the toe.

841

Produced alongside the thousands of 741s outfitted for military use was the 841, which was designed specifically for desert missions. With its "sideways" V-twin and shaft drive, it represented a radical departure from the company's typical machines.

The 45-cubic-inch engine of the 841 was a "Flathead" V-twin, but it was mounted perpendicular to normal Indian practice, with the cylinders sticking out into the airstream. Despite the unusual arrangement, many internal components were borrowed from the company's Sport Scout model. Up front was a girder-style fork, same as the 741, but the rear was fitted with the company's traditional "plunger" suspension, which the 741 lacked. Final drive was by jointed shaft, a configuration deemed more suitable for use in the abrasive desert sand. Contrary to conventional practice, the 841 had a foot-shift/ hand-clutch arrangement, as did Harley's desert bike, the XA.

Also like the XA, only about a thousand 841s were ever built. Unlike the XA, however, at least some (probably fewer than 50) saw military service. The balance were sold to civilians, most being converted for use on the street, and many can still be found at motorcycle shows across the country.

Chapter 2
Postwar European and Japanese Competition
1946–1978

While postwar motorcycles were essentially warmed-over prewar versions, some technological advancements began to appear by decade's end. But so did a flood of bikes from Europe, which gave buyers a wider choice of models—and domestic makes some serious competition. The suspension of civilian motorcycle production during World War II left a postwar void that took years to fill, and that pent-up demand helped open the market for imported machines from across the pond. Most were British, but other European imports trickled in as well.

At first, these small to midsize machines didn't pose a big threat to the heavyweight Harley-Davidsons and Indians. But as the 1950s dawned, it became apparent that the imports were siphoning off a good number of sales, and Indian couldn't stand the loss in revenue. Though it tried to counter with modern midsize motorcycles of its own, it was too little, too late, and Indian folded its tent in 1953. Harley-Davidson also countered—somewhat more successfully—but by decade's end, the trickle of imports had become a flood.

"You meet the nicest people on a Honda" proved to be one of the most successful advertising slogans of all time. Introduced in the early 1960s, it was intended to combat the negative image motorcycles—and their riders—had acquired during the 1950s. It was accompanied by a new breed of smaller, "friendlier" bikes that didn't threaten any of the established makes. But other Japanese companies soon followed Honda's lead, and the motorcycles they offered became larger and more technologically advanced. Meanwhile, the American and British makes soldiered on with few changes, and by the end of the decade, found themselves outclassed and overwhelmed.

During the 1970s, Japanese manufacturers expanded their offerings into virtually every facet of the motorcycle market. Sporting middleweights attacked the British stronghold on that segment, touring models went after Harley-Davidson's traditional customers, and hi-tech, high-performance rockets started a whole new era in motorcycling. This took a fatal toll on the British makes and changed the image of motorcycle culture to this day.

1946 Indian Chief

When Indian resumed production after the war, the four-cylinder and smaller V-twin models were relegated to history, leaving only the now-legendary V-twin Chief. These machines were similar to prewar versions; the engine remained a 74-cubic-inch "Flathead" and tank graphics were unchanged. As always, Indian Red was a popular color choice, though others—including two-tones—were available.

New, however, were girder-style coil-spring front forks adopted from Indian's radical 841 model that had been designed for desert use by the U.S. military during the war. These new forks provided a full five inches of wheel travel versus the meager two inches allowed by the previous leaf-spring design. Though the rear still featured the same plunger-type suspension, spring rates were softened. These changes resulted in an even smoother ride than before, a notable selling feature of the postwar models.

1. Two-tone color schemes could be substituted for the traditional Indian Red.

2. Another accessory was a spring-mounted sidecar, first offered in 1940, which carried fancy chrome speed lines and trim.

3. Front and rear crash bars and a locking toolbox were popular accessories of the day.

1947 Triumph Speed Twin

Like so many other early makes, the Triumph nameplate was originally affixed to a line of bicycles that came out in the late 1800s. In 1902, the company began bolting small, Belgian-made Minerva engines into the frames, and the Triumph legacy was born.

Based in Coventry, England, Triumph offered nothing but single-cylinder motorcycles in its early years. Though a two-cylinder model had gotten as far as the experimentation stage in the early 1910s, the first of Triumph's famous vertical twins didn't go on sale until much later.

In 1936, Edward Turner joined Triumph as its chief designer and general manager. He quickly went to work developing a new, lightweight two-cylinder motorcycle, and within two years the company introduced a landmark machine: the Speed Twin.

First shown in late 1937 and sold as a 1938 model, the Speed Twin featured a 500-cc engine and four-speed transmission that were carried in separate cases—a simple design that would be used in several Triumph models over the years. Blessed with decent power and a light chassis, the Speed Twin was not only the mount of choice for numerous police departments throughout Europe, but was the template used to spawn a generation of English bikes.

Modern telescopic forks handled suspension chores in front fairly well, but the sprung saddle was the only rear suspension offered, as the Speed Twin rode a rigid frame. In 1947, an optional sprung rear hub was offered, and our featured Speed Twin is so equipped. But it turned out to be a disappointment to those who ordered it, for the design allowed only minimal travel while adding a complex inner assembly of springs and related hardware.

1. Speed Twins carried a speedometer, ammeter, and light switch in the headlight bezel.

2. In the 1960s, Triumph joined other manufacturers by combining engines and transmissions into one unit, which resulted in a more compact design. Today, however, pre-unit Triumphs are highly coveted in the collector market.

3. Triumph's sprung rear hub, first offered as an option in 1947, afforded only about one inch of wheel travel—hardly a substitute for a good swingarm suspension.

1948 Harley-Davidson WL

Harley-Davidson's first "Flathead" V-twin appeared in 1929 as the Model D. Its 45-cubic-inch engine was smaller than the company's existing 61- and 74-cubic-inch "F-head" V-twins, which then became known as Big Twins. The latter switched to a "Flathead" design the following year, but those larger engines were neither as reliable nor as long-lived as the under-stressed Forty-five.

Though the Forty-five was no powerhouse, it proved to be a versatile engine that remained in production for more than four decades. During that time it served duty not only in street motorcycles, but also in three-wheeled Servi-Cars (1933–1973), military WLAs of the 1940s, and WR racing bikes of the 1940s and 1950s.

By 1948, the Forty-five was powering a street model called the WL. It looked very similar to Harley's Big Twin "Flatheads" of the era, the most noticeable visual difference being that WLs had their drive chains on the right side of the bike, while Big Twins had them on the left. Though 1948 would prove to be the final year for Big Twin "Flatheads," the WL lasted through 1951, after which it was replaced by the K-series carrying a redesigned 45-cubic-inch "Flathead" V-twin with unit construction (motor and transmission in one case).

1. Like its larger stable mates, the 45-cubic-inch WL carried a tank-mounted instrument panel.

2. It continued with Harley's hand-shift/foot-clutch arrangement, but by this time, the pattern was reversed so that first gear was closest to the rider.

3. What the Forty-five lacked in power it made up for in persistence.

4. Yet this pedestrian "Flathead" V-twin also powered one of Harley's more successful racing bikes, the WR. Intended for dirt tracks, the WR's trump card was a broad powerband that minimized the necessity to shift gears. Introduced after the war and competitive into the 1950s, it came from the factory in racing trim, meaning no lights, no horn, no fenders . . . and no brakes.

1949 BSA B33

As one of England's oldest motorcycle companies, BSA grew out of a consortium of firearms manufacturers who first expanded into bicycles, then into the fledgling "motor bicycle" market by fitting a stronger frame with a Belgian-made Minerva engine. That was in 1905; by 1910, Birmingham Small Arms was building its own 30-cubic-inch "Flathead" single, and BSA was on its way to becoming a household name.

Though the company also built large V-twins for 20 years before World War II, its stock in trade remained midsize singles. These were often available at bargain prices and thus sold in large volume. During the war, BSA supplied over 120,000 of its M20 500-cc "Flathead" singles to Allied forces, where their simple mechanicals made them reliable and easy to repair. While contests of speed were typically won by other makes, BSAs had more than their share of success in endurance races, furthering their reputation for toughness that carried far more appeal to the everyday rider.

Typical of early postwar BSAs is the B33, which arrived in 1947 with a 500-cc (30-cubic-inch) overhead-valve single. Simple and stout, it formed the basis for a series of similar machines that carried on through the 1950s. Modern telescopic forks were used in front, but early versions had a rigid frame and thus no rear suspension save for the sprung saddle.

Vertical twins joined the line after the war and became legends in their own right. And adding those to an early 1950s selection of popular small- to large-displacement singles briefly made BSA the largest motorcycle company in the world.

1. Instrumentation was simple and sparse.

2. Tall "chimney" on the side of the engine enclosed pushrods for the B33's overhead valves.

3. Notch in the rear of the fuel tank accommodates the seat.

1949 Harley-Davidson FL Hydra-Glide

After bringing out the refined "Panhead" engine the previous year, Harley's big news for 1949 was the introduction of Hydra-Glide front forks. Replacing the former leading-link forks, Hydra-Glide was a modern telescopic design that provided greater travel and a much higher level of riding comfort. However, the frame still lacked any form of rear suspension; that would take another few years to develop.

The big Harleys were now called Hydra-Glide in reference to the new forks, marking the first time they carried a name as well as a series designation. They remained available in 61-cubic-inch EL and 74-cubic-inch FL versions, and, although the latter is represented here, there was little difference in appearance.

The 1949 FL was not only more comfortable to ride, but also easier to stop due to a larger front brake. Though by this time many motorcycles were adopting foot-shift transmissions, that too was some time off for the big FL series, which still made use of a hand shifter and foot clutch.

1. Note the overload spring that could be swung into place to assist the sprung seat post when a passenger or heavier rider was aboard.

2. Tank-mounted instrument panel remained a styling element.

3. Attached to the new front end were handlebars that could be adjusted for position—a novel concept in the 1940s. Note the now-classic bucket headlight and backing plate that appeared on the Hydra-Glide.

4. Chrome trim, which in this case included speed lines, fender tips, and toolbox cover, was a popular accessory.

1951 Whizzer Pacemaker

Though perhaps more "motorbike" than "motorcycle," Whizzer's contribution to the sport centers more on what it did than what it was.

In the late 1930s, Whizzer began providing a kit whereby anyone with $80 and a bicycle could experience the thrill of motorized travel. Not fast travel, mind you, but faster than their legs alone could take them. Typically affixed to Schwinn bicycles, these kits included a two-horsepower "Flathead" engine and associated drive accessories that allowed speeds over 30 mph.

After the war, Whizzer produced a vastly more powerful engine—now a raging three horsepower—and eventually offered them in complete machines. These were Whizzer Pacemakers, which could be fitted with all manner of ritzy accessories, including "dual" exhausts. Many an enthusiast cut their riding teeth on Whizzers in the early 1950s, the experience often encouraging them to progress to larger mounts.

Whether the company's popularity helped incite the scooter trend in the late 1950s is hard to say, but if so, Whizzer became a victim of its own success. With the flood of imported scooters and mopeds that swept the country in the 1960s, Whizzer faced competition it couldn't underprice, and the company closed its doors in 1962.

1. Whizzer's initial 138-cc (8.5-cubic-inch) "Flathead" single supplied two horsepower; a later 199-cc version upped that to three.

2. Pacemakers featured a rudimentary telescopic front fork.

3. Accessories were plentiful; among those shown are chrome headlight and taillight, chrome fuel tank, speedometer, chrome luggage rack, light-up rods on rear fender, and chrome fender tips. Kits to convert any "man's balloon-tire bike" continued to be offered even after the Pacemaker was introduced.

1952 Triumph Thunderbird

Any foreign manufacturer that exports to the U.S. has to listen carefully to the changing demands of the marketplace, and that's just what Triumph did when it released the 6T in 1950. While the company's offerings were generally well received in postwar America, there was a cry for more power from those accustomed to large displacement Indians and Harley-Davidsons. And though the 6T's 650-cc engine was barely half the size of the thunderous V-twins of those rivals, it was at least a step in the right direction.

Triumph's popular Speed Twin was the basis for the 6T, and their engines looked the same from the outside. But it was what was inside that made the difference: Some minor modifications and an extra 150 ccs of displacement netted eight more horsepower, raising the total to 34.

New, too, was the styling. A monotone paint scheme bathed the frame, tanks, forks, fenders, and even wheel rims in the same color, while new badges and a luggage rack graced the fuel tank. The headlamp was housed in a streamlined nacelle that tapered into the telescopic front forks, and speed lines were added to fenders, the nacelle, and as part of the badge on the fuel tank.

As was Triumph's custom, the 6T was given a "stage name" in addition to its alphanumeric designation, and Thunderbird became the chosen moniker—this, of course, years before it was applied to Ford's two-seat sports car.

1. Pre-unit Triumphs, in which the engine and transmission were housed in separate cases, had an oil tank mounted beneath the seat. Here, the transmission is below the oil tank.

2. While modern telescopic forks were found in front, some Triumphs of the era used a rigid rear frame with a sprung hub in the rear wheel.

3. The sprung hub was a complex mechanical device that allowed only about one inch of wheel travel—hardly worth the effort.

1953 Indian Chief

Though Indian had enjoyed a long and rich history, financial problems beset the company in the early 1950s. Attempts at postwar singles and vertical twins intended to compete with the machines from Europe ultimately proved unsuccessful, and their development had cost the company dearly.

By 1953, the sole surviving Indian was the V-twin Chief, and despite Indian's monetary crisis, it had seen a fair number of updates during the postwar years. Modern telescopic forks replaced the girder front end in 1950, when the 74-cubic-inch V-twin was enlarged to 80 cubic inches. In 1952, the front fender was trimmed to a thinner contour and a cowling was added on top of the forks.

The Chief's "Flathead" V-twin was considered somewhat archaic compared to Harley-Davidson's overhead-valve engines, but the Indian used a more modern ignition system. Whereas Harleys had a single coil that fired both plugs at the same time once per revolution (one plug firing needlessly), Indian used an automotive-type distributor that fired each plug only on its cylinder's power stroke. This was hardly an overwhelming advantage, however.

According to factory records, 700 Chiefs were built in 1952, while only 600 were completed in 1953. After that, the Chief—and Indian along with it—was relegated to history, leaving Harley-Davidson the sole surviving American motorcycle manufacturer.

With its massive skirted fenders, locomotive-like torque, and "last-of-the-breed" heritage, the 1953 Chief is surely one of the most collectible of Indians. It represents both the crowning achievement and the sorrowful end of a company that gave generations of motorcyclists some of their fondest memories.

1. Indian enlarged its 74-cubic-inch V-twin to 80 inches in 1950, and those models received a signifying decal on their fuel tanks.

2. The rider's view was dominated by chrome.

3. By 1953, the Chief carried acres of sheet metal, the latest addition being a cowling mounted behind the headlight. Note the running light on the front fender.

1954 AJS

In England, during the early 1900s, the Stevens brothers built engines for use in the frames of other manufacturers. In 1909, the initials of the oldest brother, Albert John Stevens, would appear on their first complete motorcycle. AJS built singles and V-twins in the years before World War II, and took home several trophies in the early days of TT racing, which would help sales for many years.

AJS continued as an independent manufacturer until 1931, when financial woes forced it to join forces with the Matchless Company to form Associated Motor Cycles (AMC). Although both lines continued under their own names, they became synonymous in construction, differing only in badging and trim.

The 16M was the first postwar AJS to be released. Its mechanical roots dated back to the models of 1935, though improvements had been implemented in the intervening years. The 16M breathed through larger Amal carbs in 1954, and also had a new automatic ignition advance mechanism that made riding more pleasant. To make room for this revision, a new side cover was installed, easily identified by a hump in its surface.

In the postwar era, AJS offered singles and, after 1949, vertical twins. Much like early Fords, AJS cycles of the 1950s were always finished in black, as were their Matchless siblings. However, AJS models wore gold striping, while their Matchless counterparts were trimmed with silver. This was hardly enough to differentiate the two, however, and loyalties to both brands faded.

AMC had purchased ailing Norton in 1952, but resisted the temptation to roll that marque into the same badge-engineering program as AJS/Matchless—until 1964, that is. First chassis components and then engines were shared, none of which helped sales of any of the makes, and AMC folded in 1966. Matchless was gone for good, but Norton continued under Norton/Villiers, which sold an AJS badged dirt bike into the 1970s.

1. Though AJS and Matchless machines were virtually identical mechanically, AJS versions had distinct generator-drive covers and wore gold trim rather than silver.

2. Cap-like protrusion in the left-side primary cover ahead of the foot peg housed the new-for-1954 automatic ignition advance.

3. Period AJS/Matchless ad touts the availability of replacement parts, a concern among prospective buyers of foreign machines.

1954 Harley-Davidson FL Hydra-Glide

With the demise of Indian in 1953, Harley-Davidson entered the 1954 model year as the sole surviving American motorcycle manufacturer. While that might seem like a cause for celebration in Milwaukee, the truth was that Harley's fortunes were in doubt as well, since bikes from across the pond—particularly England—were becoming as much a threat as Indian ever was.

What the company did celebrate that year was its 50th anniversary. Why this didn't take place the year before (the company having been founded in 1903) is a mystery, but all the 1954 models wore special medallions on their front fenders to commemorate the occasion.

The Anniversary Yellow FL shown sports the hand-clutch/foot-shift arrangement introduced in 1952, though traditionalists—and police departments—could still order one with hand shift. Many preferred the older setup because the bike could be left running with the transmission in gear and the clutch disengaged thanks to the "rocking" clutch pedal.

In addition to the commemorative front fender badge, the 50th anniversary FLs were shown with a new trumpet-style horn. This example is fitted with the optional color-matched handgrips and kick-start pedal. Two-tone paint (with the tank and fenders in different colors) was also optional.

FL models accounted for nearly half of all Harleys sold in 1954. Total sales were down from the previous year, and wouldn't rebound until 1957, when the import-fighting Sportster was introduced.

1. The FL's "Panhead" V-twin displaced 74 cubic inches; the similar EL model, with a 61-cubic-inch engine, was discontinued after 1952.

2. For unknown reasons, Harley-Davidson celebrated its 50th anniversary in 1954, rather than 1953, which would have reflected the company's 1903 founding. Future celebrations would be based on the founding date.

3. The big Harleys were always popular with law enforcement. This example is fitted with the "old" hand-shift/foot-clutch arrangement that was still available, largely because it remained popular with police departments. Note the Motorola speaker and microphone by the handlebars; the transceiver was carried in the left saddlebag.

4. An FL with the optional two-tone paint shows off the also-optional dual exhausts, dual spotlights, and rear luggage carrier.

1956 Simplex Automatic

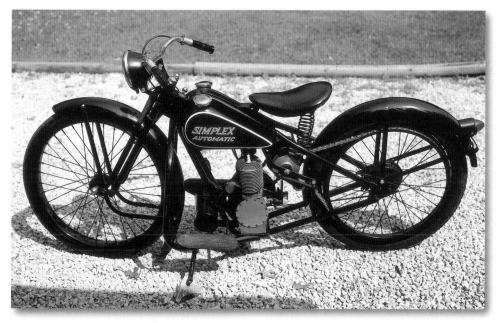

The Simplex Automatic shown here was designed and built in the U.S. Several other manufacturers used the Simplex name, but they were based in Holland, Italy, and England. Hailing from New Orleans, Louisiana, the Simplex was the brainchild of Mr. Paul Treen, who started the company in the late 1920s with a $25 investment. A draftsman by trade and inventor by nature, the Simplex was a natural extension of his abilities and vision.

Surprisingly, it was the only motorcycle ever built in the southern part of the country. The first Simplex arrived in 1935, and as the name implied, was built with simplicity in mind. Its 125-cc engine powered the rear wheel through a direct-drive arrangement, eliminating the complexity (and expense) of a transmission and clutch.

Later models, however, added more features. The Simplex Automatic was fitted with an automatic clutch and variable transmission. Furthermore, its two-stroke engine incorporated a rotary valve that was quite unusual for the period. Lightweight and efficient design combined to return a claimed 100 mpg.

Simplex cycles were built until 1960. During their life span, revisions were frequent thanks to Mr. Treen's tireless efforts to improve on his simple motorcycle design. The company continued to build go-carts for several years after motorcycle production ceased.

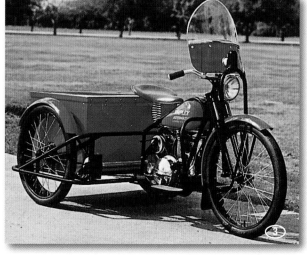

1. A single seat spring provided "rear" suspension. Power was routed through an automatic clutch to a variable transmission and then on to the rear wheel. Rather than a chain or plain belt, the Simplex used "linked" belts to transfer driving forces.

2. Evidently, top speed was insufficient to warrant a speedometer. Leading-link front-suspension design dated from the earliest days of motorcycling.

3. Fitted with three wheels and a cargo box (similar to Harley-Davidson's larger Servi-Car), the Simplex made a handy around town runabout. This example is equipped with a tow bar and was popular with service stations, the idea being that it could be towed behind a customer's car being delivered after service work, and then ridden back to the garage.

1957 Ariel 4G Mk II

Ariel was one of the British motorcycle industry's more adventurous manufacturers. Begun in 1902, the company produced an array of singles and twins of both two- and four-stroke design, but it is an unusual four-cylinder model that is perhaps best remembered.

During the 1920s, Ariel's Edward Turner had dreams of changing the world of motorcycling. For many years, twin-cylinder engines were the power plant of choice, but Turner had grander ideas. Envisioning a four-cylinder engine that would fit neatly into a typical frame, he devised the unusual "Square Four" design. It used two crankshafts geared together and four cylinders arranged in a square pattern, with a pair of pistons tied to each crankshaft.

Displacing 500 ccs, the first Ariel "Square Four" appeared in 1931, venting its exhaust through only two pipes. The four was enlarged to 600 ccs in 1932, and then to 1000 ccs in 1936. In 1953, the Mk II version appeared, carrying a four-pipe exhaust system and an alloy block in place of the previous iron version.

Some other changes were evident by this time as well. The tank-mounted instrument panel was eliminated and the gauges were now mounted atop the wide headlight nacelle. A new plunger rear suspension provided a softer ride, but needed fresh lubrication every 250 miles. The girder front fork had been converted to telescopic in 1946 and went largely untouched.

Turner left Ariel to join Triumph in the 1930s, where his talents in developing the Speed Twin helped revive the ailing concern. Ariel's success with the "Square Four" continued through the 1950s, after which the company concentrated on medium-displacement two-strokes that were a cross between a scooter and a motorcycle.

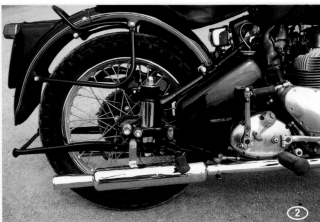

1. Instruments were originally mounted on top of the fuel tank, but were later moved to the top of the steering head and, in the 1950s, to the top of the headlight nacelle, as shown here.

2. Ariel's unique "Square Four", sometimes referred to as the "Squariel," originally had only two exhaust pipes exiting the four-cylinder engine, making it look like just a "fat" twin; a four-pipe setup arrived with the Mk II version of 1953.

3. Plunger-type rear suspension design was shared with, among others, Indian.

1957 Harley-Davidson XL Sportster

Since the K series introduced in 1952 was getting a lukewarm reception—not to mention regularly beaten by smaller British twins—Harley-Davidson introduced the famed Sportster in 1957. With overhead valves topping a 55-cubic-inch V-twin, the Sportster lived up to its name, proving somewhat quicker than its predecessor.

Save for its overhead-valve engine, the Sportster looked similar to the final KH models—because it was. Telescopic front forks and swingarm rear suspension carried over, as did most styling elements save the two-tone paint treatment and tank badge. Even the engine's primary case looked familiar, the new one differing only in that it had *SPORTSTER* cast into its side.

Like the K-series bikes, Sportsters had their shifters and drive chains on the right, whereas Harley's big FLs had them on the left. In the case of the shifters in particular, this might seem odd, as riders moving up would have to learn to shift with the other foot. But the XL was mimicking British makes, which were its intended target.

1. Instrument panels held a simple speedometer, while oil pressure and generator warning lights were built into the headlight housing.

2. At first glance, only the cylinder barrels and heads told onlookers this wasn't a KH—well, those and the bold *SPORTSTER* cast into the primary cover.

3. Our featured example is painted Pepper Red over black; buyers could request the colors to be reversed. Backing the headlight was a cover similar to that used on Harley's big FLs.

1958 Harley-Davidson FL Duo-Glide

Finally, after decades of relying only on a sprung saddle for "rear" suspension, the big Harleys adopted a modern swingarm with coil-over shocks in 1958. With that, the Hydra-Glide became the Duo-Glide, upping the ante in the touring market.

Two versions of the Big Twin continued to be offered: The milder, low-compression FL engine ran cooler and was easier to kick over than the hopped-up FLH, making it better suited to around-town driving. Still sized at 1200 ccs (74 cubic inches), period Big Twins were advertised at 53–55 horsepower in the FL, and 58–60 in the FLH.

Despite the new rear suspension, a sprung seat post remained standard, providing what Harley termed "the Glide Ride." Of course, nearly 600 lb worth of bump-flattening weight didn't hurt, either.

1. Chrome accessories abounded to put an FL out front in the "see and be seen" sweepstakes.

2. "Be seen" items included chrome crash bars, fender tips, rear grab bar, and instrument panel surround.

3. As far as "seeing" is concerned, well, three headlights and a windshield should do the trick.

1959 Ariel Leader

Prior to the unveiling of the Leader, Ariel had been best known for its four-stroke singles, twins, and the unique "Square Four." But after exhaustive market research, the company decided it was time to change direction.

What appeared in July 1958 was a combination of several new technologies for Ariel, primarily the use of a 250-cc two-stroke engine, pressed-steel frame, and odd-looking trailing-link front forks. The enclosed styling allowed for a chassis structure that stored fuel beneath the seat, while the "tank" served as a convenient storage area.

Another interesting aspect of the Leader was the long list of options available. As a result, few of the 22,000 produced were exactly the same. Color choices included Oriental Blue or Cherry Red with Admiral Gray accents, and the model featured sports the optional side bags and rear luggage rack.

By 1959, Ariel had put all its cards into the Leader, having dropped the "Square Four" that year. A cheaper, stripped Arrow model followed, as did a Golden Arrow "sport" version. But the deck was stacked against it by this time as Japanese imports flooded the market, and Ariel folded its hand in 1965.

1. Despite its rather odd looks, the Leader was a functional vehicle that offered many useful features and options. The enclosed body made cleaning a snap, and the full fairing and windshield made cool-weather riding more bearable.

2. Instrument panel included a speedometer, ammeter, and of all things, a clock.

3. Optional luggage rack and side bags add carrying capacity.

4. Note the wild paisley seat cover.

1965 BMW R-27

Starting out as a builder of aircraft during World War I, Bayerische Motoren Werke turned to motorcycles after the hostilities ceased. Despite the change in products, the company's circular blue-and-white logo—which depicts spinning propeller blades—was retained, and remains to this day.

BMW motorcycles have long been synonymous with horizontal twins and shaft drive, which were used on the very first examples. However, the company also produced smaller single-cylinder machines for many years, and added inline threes and fours in the 1980s.

Early BMWs had stamped-steel frames, and the company was among the first to use telescopic forks starting in 1935. During World War II, Germany purchased thousands of V-twin sidecar-equipped outfits from BMW, and the motorcycle's design prompted the U.S. to commission Harley-Davidson and Indian to build near copies, though only a couple thousand were produced and only a handful saw service.

BMW's first shaft-drive singles arrived in 1925 to satisfy the demand for smaller bikes. Like other BMWs of the day, they used a trailing-link front suspension and rigid frame, switching to telescopic forks in 1935 and a plunger rear suspension in 1938.

In 1955, BMW replaced its telescopic front end with an Earles fork, which resembles a swingarm rear suspension in design. In single-cylinder 250-cc form, this model was designated the R-26. Most mechanical components were carried over from the R-26 to the R-27 shown here. This example has individual "swinging saddles" in lieu of the standard two-up seat, the former supposedly providing more rider and passenger comfort.

Though it grew in popularity throughout its seven-year production run, the R-27 would be dropped after 1967. BMW would not offer another single until the early 1990s, when an Italian-built on/off-road model powered by a Rotax engine was introduced.

1. BMWs of the era sported Earles-type forks, which provided a very smooth ride; a swingarm pivoted off a rigid fork, with coil-over shocks mounted between the axle and the top of the fork, cushioning bumps.

2. Optional rider and passenger "swinging saddles" extended coil springs on impact.

3. R-27s were occasionally fitted with sidecars, though the bike was somewhat underpowered for this purpose. This one carries the standard one-piece saddle.

1965 DKW Hummel 155

DKW, Das Kleine Wunder ("The Little Wonder"), began assembling powered cycles in 1919, and in 1932 became a partner in the Auto Union conglomerate. Most of DKW's earlier units were built with engines of at least 98 ccs of displacement, but they were always two-stroke designs.

Upon the public introduction of the Hummel 155, the European motoring press dubbed it the "Tin Banana." Its appearance was a radical departure from any contemporary offerings. In addition to the swoopy, avant-garde bodywork, the Hummel set itself apart from the competition by having a three-speed gearbox. With only a 50-cc engine producing 4.2 horsepower, the 155 was able to cruise at 45 mph. This example is fitted with a conventional foot shifter, though a hand shifter was available as an option.

The art-deco styling might have been a big hit in the U.S., but the Hummel was never exported. Being readily available across Europe was not enough to elicit strong demand, and it never sold in great numbers.

1. Though the Hummel may look whimsical to some, its art-deco styling certainly makes it stand out. Front suspension used an Earles-type fork, much like contemporary BMWs.

2. The headlight nacelle redefines the term "streamlined."

3. Front suspension used an Earles-type fork, much like contemporary BMWs.

4. A "Shredder" face shield covers the tiny 50-cc cylinder.

1965 Harley-Davidson FL Electra-Glide

For Harley-Davidson, 1965 marked the end of an era. The Electra-Glide, with its electric starter, made its debut, but it would be the last year for the famous "Panhead" V-twin that was introduced in 1948. That engine had received some modifications over the years, a significant one coming in 1963 with external oil lines that improved lubrication to the cylinder heads. Along with the electric starter came 12-volt electrics to replace the previous 6-volt system, which in turn brought a bigger battery hidden beneath a large battery case on the right side. That, along with the bold *Electra-Glide* script on the front fender, makes it easy to distinguish this model from earlier FLs.

The Electra-Glide pictured has the standard exhaust system that had both cylinders exhausting to the right into a single muffler; optional was a dual-muffler system where the exhaust from the front cylinder exited to the right, while that from the rear cylinder exited to the left, both terminating in their own distinctive fishtail muffler. Also optional was the old hand-shift/foot-clutch arrangement that was so popular with police departments. Though a curb weight of more than 700 lb restricted performance somewhat, the Electra-Glide was a popular touring mount in its day, as the electric starter alleviated the problem of having to kick start the big V-twin—which had become no easy task. And that, combined with being the last model fitted with the venerable "Panhead" engine, has made it a highly coveted collectible.

1. The Electra-Glide's mammoth headlight bezel first appeared in 1960, and has become yet another Harley trademark still in use on some models today.

2. Script on the front fender advertised the model's new electric starter, which is mounted at the forward end of the crankcase between the front cylinder and exhaust pipe.

3. Driver's view of the Electra-Glide was dominated by chrome.

1966 Suzuki T10

The Suzuki we know today started out in 1909 building an entirely different sort of machine. Silk production was a major industry in Japan at the time, and the company got its start making silk looms. Though Suzuki built an experimental engine in the late 1930s with an eye toward production, World War II intervened.

After the war, the company switched to heaters and farm machinery, and it wasn't until 1952 that the engine resurfaced. This came in the form of a small 36-cc two-stroke that could be fitted to a bicycle, and Suzuki was on the road.

Production of a complete 90-cc motorbike began in 1954, and Suzuki was one of the first companies to introduce oil injection on its two-strokes, which relieved riders of having to mix the gas and oil themselves. In 1963, Suzuki built a road-going version of a 250-cc two-stroke twin that had been raced in the 1950s, calling it the T10.

Along with oil injection, the T10 was fitted with such luxuries as electric start, hydraulic rear brake, turn signals (not yet universal), and an enclosed drive chain. Its pressed-steel frame resulted in flowing contours aft of the chrome-sided fuel tank, and that, along with 17-inch wheels, tire-hugging front fender, and telescopic front forks, gave the T10 a contemporary look. Performance was not a priority, the T10 being aimed at commuters with its mild-mannered engine boasting a broad torque range. That philosophy, however, was about to change.

1. Aimed more at luxury than performance, the T10 included only a speedometer in its headlight-mounted instrument panel.

2. Twin-cylinder two-stroke featured oil injection, an unusual convenience at the time.

3. An enclosed drive chain helped keep the bike—and the rider—free from messy chain-lube splatters.

4. Suzuki made a point in advertising that the odd-shaped headlight was brighter than most, aiding nighttime safety.

1969 Honda CB750

In June of 1968, Honda dropped the gauntlet that would forever change the world of motorcycling. The CB750 Four offered a combination of hardware never before seen on a single machine. At the heart of the CB750 was an inline four-cylinder engine with single overhead cam, four carburetors, prominent four-into-four exhaust, and 67 horsepower at 8,000 rpm. It put out a good 15-percent more power than BSA's new 750-cc Rocket 3 and at just under 500 lb, weighed about the same. It's not hard to guess which was quicker.

But it wasn't just the four-cylinder engine that caused such a stir; though most contemporary competitors were twins, fours had been offered by several manufacturers in the past. No, it was the fact that four-cylinder power and smoothness was joined by a five-speed gearbox, electric starter, and a front disc brake—the first ever on a street machine—all at a reasonable price.

The first CB750s were produced with sand-cast cases that had a rough finish; later models had smoother castings. Those early sand-cast models, such as the bike pictured, have become the most valuable to collectors.

By 1970, Dick Mann had piloted a race-prepped CB750 into the winner's circle at Daytona, and the world of aftermarket hop-up equipment came alive. The CB750 is also credited with casting the mold for what would later be called the "Universal Japanese Motorcycle," a breed of machines that would bring the bikes of England to their collective knees.

1. For the first time on a production bike, a front-disc brake was standard equipment—fitting, given the whopping speed potential, which was claimed to be 130 mph.

2. With 67 horsepower at 8,000 rpm, the CB750's four-cylinder engine was both powerful and smooth.

3. Redline was 8,500 rpm.

1970 Ducati 350 Scrambler

Starting out as an electronics firm in the 1920s, Ducati lost everything in World War II and had to rebuild. As in many other countries, Italy was in need of personal transport, so the company began producing a small engine that could be mounted on a bicycle. However, it differed from most others of its kind in being a four stroke with an integral two-speed transmission.

By the early 1950s, Ducati was building complete motorcycles, though only small, pedestrian ones. This changed in 1955 when a 98-cc single appeared with bevel-driven overhead cam, a layout that would define Ducati engines for the next few decades. It was instantly successful in racing, and led to larger and more powerful machines.

Another Ducati trademark was desmodromic valve actuation, which was introduced on a 125-cc racer in 1956. Instead of using springs to close the valves, which often "floated" at high rpm, they were closed mechanically. This feature didn't show up on production models until the late 1960s, but these 250- and 350-cc singles were quick bikes indeed, and a 450 that followed was even quicker. However, only the sporting Ducatis got the "desmo" valvetrain; tamer models used valve springs.

The 350 Scrambler featured here was considered one of the "tamer" models, though it was still fast for a bike of its size. Singles lasted until 1973, by which time the V-twins introduced two years earlier had taken over the showrooms.

1. As with many other bikes of the era, the Scrambler's speedometer was mounted in the headlight housing, though the needle's direction of travel was reversed from common practice.

2. Though the Scrambler didn't carry Ducati's famed desmodromic valvetrain, like all Ducati four-strokes of the period, it did have bevel-gear cam drive; one of the gears is evident inside the black ring at the top of the engine.

1972 Kawasaki H2 750 Mach IV

Founded in the late 1800s, Kawasaki has been into everything from planes to trains to shipping. Though it supplied small motorcycle engines (complete with transmissions) to other manufacturers since just after World War II, Kawasaki did not offer its own bikes until 1960. But this new segment of the company advanced—and grew—quickly.

One of the manufacturers using those small engines was Meguro, which Kawasaki bought out in the early 1960s. The first machines that wore Kawasaki badges were 125-cc commuter bikes, which didn't go over well when the company exported them to the United States. But Meguro had also been building a 650-cc four-stroke overhead-valve twin under license from BSA (the English company's old pre-unit model), and this met with a fair degree of success in the U.S. when introduced as the W1 in 1966. But better—and faster—models were yet to come.

First up was a 250-cc two-stroke twin called the Samurai, which certainly represented an about-face in philosophy from the W1. Fitted with rotary disc valves, it was a hot little number, and the temperature was raised further by the 350-cc Avenger that followed. And then came the big one.

In the midst of numerous new "superbikes" being introduced by Triumph, BSA, and Honda, the 500-cc H1 Mach III two-stroke triple stood out as a ferocious performer at a cut-rate price. Light and very powerful, with 60 horses that seemed to lie in wait and then suddenly stampede when the revs built up, rumors abounded of Mach IIIs that reared up and threw their riders off on the first test drives. But in the raging superbike wars, "too much" was still not enough.

Enter the 750-cc H2 Mach IV. With 74 horsepower on tap, it was even more fearsome than the Mach III. And not surprisingly, it inherited several of its parent's flaws, namely squirrely handling, a propensity to wheelie, and horrific fuel mileage. So although it was perhaps the ultimate performance two-stroke of the day, the market—and Kawasaki—would soon be drifting toward more civilized four-strokes.

1. Peaky power output of the Mach IV's 750-cc triple often proved troublesome for the unwary.

2. Big front disc was reassuring given the bike's 130-mph speed potential, but did little good when the front wheel was in the air.

3. Three-pipe exhaust system mounted two pipes on one side, one on the other.

1973 Kawasaki Z-1

After Honda introduced the CB750 in 1969, other Japanese manufacturers scrambled to best the effort. One of the most notable outcomes of this mad dash was Kawasaki's Z-1.

Kawasaki had made its mark in the U.S. with its fast but frightening two-stroke triples, but Honda's success with its more civilized CB750 Four did not go unnoticed. The market was beginning to lean away from two-strokes in general, and Kawasaki wanted to maintain its performance image while offering a more road-able four-stroke machine. Introduced in 1973, the Z-1 boasted a 903-cc double-overhead-cam inline four that significantly upped the performance ante. That engine soon became the benchmark other companies would aim to beat, and it proved to be a bulletproof design that continues to be a dominant force in racing circles to this day.

In contrast to the strong-running powerplant, the chassis of the Z-1 was notoriously unstable. Several aftermarket manufacturers quickly devised more competent frame designs that could be filled with Z-1 power.

No color options were offered for the U.S. market, all Z-1s being painted brown with orange accents. Not considered a particularly appealing combination at the time, many early Z-1s received custom paint treatments shortly after leaving the showroom.

1. Kawasaki wanted to trump Honda's hand, and did so with a state-of-the-art 900-cc double-overhead-cam four producing 82 horsepower—15 more than the Honda—that could rev to a stratospheric (for the time) 9,000 rpm.

2. It was also decidedly more docile and forgiving than Kawasaki's earlier two-stroke machines. Kawasaki called it "the ultimate way to come out ahead...."

The motorcycle has come a long way. From A to Z-1: the ultimate way to come out ahead on a Kawasaki.

Z-1 900cc

More muscle than any other 750 touring bike.   Newest version of the famous Mach III.

1975 Triumph Trident

In an attempt to fend off the attack of Japanese exports to the lucrative U.S. market, Triumph and BSA released a pair of three-cylinder models. The Triumph T150 Trident and BSA Rocket 3 were introduced in the States during the summer of 1968.

Despite the fact that the two companies had joined forces in 1951 and the motorcycles themselves were similar in specification, the Trident and Rocket 3 differed in many respects. Styling was unique to each, and even the engines were slightly different: the Trident had vertically mounted cylinders, while those on the Rocket 3 were canted forward a bit.

While both were considered decent motorcycles that challenged the best in terms of performance, their strengths paled with the introduction of Honda's 750 Four a few months later. Both British bikes received minor updates in subsequent years, but the Rocket 3 dropped out of the picture in 1973 (along with BSA itself), while the Trident got an overhaul.

The revised Trident, called the T160, carried several new features. The most obvious change was the adoption of inclined cylinders that allowed for a slightly lower profile. The engine also was fitted with more durable internal hardware and gained an electric starter. To appeal to American tastes (and laws), the shift lever was moved to the left side of the bike. A 10-inch disc brake finally appeared up front to replace the antiquated drum.

Unfortunately for Triumph, the superbike ante had been raised by the likes of Kawasaki's new Z-1, and though certainly improved, the Trident just didn't measure up. Furthermore, the displacement of its Bonneville twin-cylinder sibling had been increased to the same 750 ccs in 1973, and few buyers could justify the Trident's higher price.

As a result, Triumph's triple faded from the scene after 1976, though the name was revived in 1990 for a more modern, water-cooled, three-cylinder machine to be produced by a new Triumph corporation.

1. The second-generation Trident received some subtle changes, including an electric starter and cylinders that went from vertical to slightly inclined. The center exhaust port was split, allowing the center pipe to join with each of the outer ones, and each pair then routed into its own muffler.

2. Featured here, the motorcycle got a left-side shifter.

3. The X-75, designed by Craig Vetter of fairing fame, was a styling exercise based on the Trident. It featured sleek, cafe-racer bodywork and a prominent three-muffler exhaust system. A fair number were sold through Triumph dealers, and they are very valuable today.

1977 Ducati 900SS

Ducati's domination on the racetracks across Europe has led to the development of some exceptional road-going machines. With the debut of the 750SS and its desmodromic valvetrain in 1974, Ducati reached a new plateau of performance. Easily able to reach velocities in excess of 120 mph in a single bound, the 750SS reintroduced the world to Italian superbikes.

In 1976, a more powerful version of the SS appeared. Based on the non-desmodromic 860GT introduced in late 1973, the new 900SS added desmodromics to the larger engine, pushing the performance envelope even further.

With a top speed of over 140 mph, the 900SS was as fast as anything the Japanese had to offer. The carefully sculpted steel fuel tank was surrounded by a bullet-shaped half fairing, and the solo saddle was backed by an aerodynamic tailpiece. Together, these elements created a true racing image for the 900SS, which was only strengthened when Mike Hailwood rode a race-prepped version to victory at the Isle of Man TT.

1. The tachometer shows an 8,000-rpm redline—quite high for a large-displacement twin.

2. Dual ventilated front disc brakes provided needed reassurance given the bike's high-speed potential.

3. The 900SS, introduced in 1976, carried an 860-cc V-twin fitted with Ducati's famous desmodromic valvetrain, which closed the valves mechanically rather than with springs; this virtually eliminated high-rpm valve float. Note that the cooling fins on the forward cylinder run in a different direction than those on the rear cylinder due to the direction of air flow.

1978 Harley-Davidson FXS

Harley-Davidson's first "factory custom" was released in 1971, setting the stage for many more to follow. Called the FX Super-Glide, it combined the frame and engine from the big FL-series twins with the front forks and other trim pieces from the XL Sportster—hence the FX designation.

In the middle of 1977, Harley rolled out the FXS Low Rider. Like the Super-Glide, it was based on the big FL series frame with a 74-cubic-inch V-twin. With a seat height of only 27 inches, the FXS fit almost any rider. In looks and concept, it contrasted sharply with Harley's other new entry for 1977, the XLCR. While the Sportster-based XLCR was square and sporty, the FXS had a low, muscular flow to its profile.

In 1978, the Low Rider's first full year of production, it outsold all other models in Harley's line, accounting for nearly 20 percent of total sales. The FXS was initially sold only in metallic gray with orange script, but black and white were offered late in the model year.

On the FXS, fuel is stored in the split "Fat Bob" tanks, which give the bike a substantial look. The 1978 version still carried both kick and electric starters, and the final drive was handled with a multi-row chain.

Though it was the first full year for the Low Rider, 1978 turned out to be the last year for the venerable 74-cubic-inch V-twin, as Harley increased the displacement to 80 cubic inches for 1979.

1. A matte-black finish was used on the instrument panel and upper tank trim.

2. Continuing the formula used for the original Super-Glide of 1971, the first Low Rider featured the frame and engine from the FL-series Big Twins supported by the front end of the smaller XL Sportster models. Big 74-cubic-inch V-twin exhaled through a two-into-one header.

Chapter 3
Customization and Variation Run the Market
1979–2017

As Japanese manufacturers sought to broaden their product ranges, they looked to established offerings for inspiration—and tried to outdo them. Italian makes, most notably Ducati, were the influence for sport bikes (essentially "super" bikes with full fairings), while Harley-Davidsons served as the template for cruisers. Add to these a host of touring bikes, moto-crossers, enduros (which evolved from scramblers), along with traditionally styled machines, and the available choices became nearly limitless.

The various niches—standards, sport bikes, cruisers, touring bikes, and enduros—produced some crossover models combining elements of different classes. One of the most popular was the "naked" bike, essentially a sport bike shorn of its fiberglass fairing, thus exposing its motor and exotic frame. These new models resulted in broader product lines—and more choices for consumers.

As motorcycling entered the 21st century, the popularity of the sport was on the rise. Becoming a larger part of the scene were factory-built choppers offered by numerous independent companies. In many ways these "backyard builders" mimicked those that started the motorcycle craze more than a century before. Some offer a line of models, others custom-build each bike to the customer's specifications, but nearly all are powered by proprietary V-twin motors.

In the end, it doesn't really matter what kind of bike is chosen; it's the excitement of the ride that counts. And if the current level of enthusiasm is any indication, the sport of motorcycling will be going strong well into the next century.

1981 Harley-Davidson Heritage Edition

Harley-Davidson celebrated its 75th Anniversary in 1978, and one of the product highlights of that year was the return of an 80-cubic-inch V-twin, absent from the line since World War II. Soon afterward, the "retro" look came into vogue at Harley-Davidson, a styling trend that continues to this day. One of the first products to combine these two features was the 1981 Heritage Edition.

Carrying a two-place saddle, headlight nacelle, green and orange paint, and other features seen on classic Harleys of yesteryear (but equipped with modern suspension and brakes), only 784 Heritage Editions were built for 1981, and the model did not return in 1982. With its time-honored styling and low production numbers, the Heritage itself has now become a coveted classic.

But perhaps overshadowing any of Harley-Davidson's product offerings in 1981 was a much larger event that took place in June of that year. After more than a decade under the AMF banner, a group of Harley-Davidson employees arranged financing and bought back the company. While production and profits both increased under AMF, quality didn't. After the buyout, employees and enthusiasts alike took a new pride in Harley-Davidson.

1. By this time, Harley had moved the choke knob to a more convenient location on the instrument panel, where the owner's name could be engraved on a special Heritage Edition plaque.

2. A mixture of old and new graced the fuel tank; old-style lettering, but with the AMF logo. The latter would be the first thing to go after employees bought Harley-Davidson back from AMF in the summer of 1981.

3. A Heritage Edition emblem also graced the engine's primary cover.

4. For those who might wonder what to call the green and orange dresser, the front fender spelled it out for them.

1983 Honda CX650T

The sport bike battle had been raging for a good ten years when Honda introduced a new and innovative competitor: the CX500 Turbo. Not only was it the world's first turbocharged production bike, it also featured fuel injection and the most radical fairing yet seen on a motorcycle.

The Turbo's powerplant was based on the water-cooled V-twin with four pushrod-operated overhead valves per cylinder used in the shaft-drive CX500 introduced a few years earlier—itself a groundbreaking design. The base engine also was used in the Silver Wing, a touring machine aimed at being the Gold Wing's little brother, and a Custom model with "chopper" styling.

In 1983, both versions of the V-twin were bumped to 650 ccs. For the new CX650 Turbo, that meant a boost from 77 to 97 horsepower, making it one of the more powerful motorcycles available that year. Otherwise, it was mostly a carryover from the CX500 Turbo, although the color scheme was changed from pearlescent eggshell with red and black accents to the pearlescent white with red and blue trim as shown on our featured bike.

With their complex fuel injection systems and related sensors and actuators, the CX Turbos carried high prices and were a nightmare for shade-tree mechanics. And while spiraling insurance rates were affecting all performance bikes, many insurers looked unfavorably at turbocharged models in particular, assessing them with exorbitant premiums. So although the whistle of the turbo and resulting kick of acceleration boiled the adrenaline of those who rode one, the CX650 Turbo—along with the imitators that soon followed—sadly suffered a premature extinction.

1. The CX's V-twin was unusual in that each of the head's four valves were operated by pushrods rather than overhead cams. Mounted "sideways" in the frame à la Moto Guzzi, the rather pedestrian engine grew significantly stronger with the addition of electronic fuel injection and a turbocharger.

2. More sedate versions of the CX sold far better than the complicated and expensive Turbo.

1985 Yamaha RZ 500

In the early 1980s, the marketing department at Yamaha sensed the need for an all-out performance machine. It had to be light in weight, look and behave like a Gran Prix bike, and be within budgetary guidelines. After several years of development, the RZ 500 shot out the Yamaha factory doors.

In a brash deviation from the norm, the RZ was powered by a 499-cc "square" four-cylinder two-stroke with twin cranks and liquid cooling. Somewhat more conventional was a chassis formed from square-section aluminum-alloy tubing. This choice of material allowed for superb stiffness matched with light weight.

The RZ's extraordinary performance and handling were actually seen as detriments to the average rider, and sales of Yamaha's little pocket rocket were poor. Placed in the proper hands, it was a potent weapon on the track, but unfortunately a handful around town. Furthermore, the two-stroke powerplant excluded the RZ 500 from the list of machines available for sale in the United States, though several examples managed to find their way in anyhow.

1. Wild twin-crank four-cylinder two-stroke was tame at low revs, but exploded to life as it neared its 10,000-rpm redline. A six-speed gearbox allowed the rider to keep the peaky two-stroke within its narrow power range.

2. Exhaust flowed through four pipes; two in the normal position, two more jutting from either side of the taillight. Bulbous expansion chambers helped produce more power.

3. Adjustable anti-dive mechanism on the forks was triggered by application of the front brakes.

1986 Ducati 750 F1 Montjuich

Ducati entered the motorcycle market after World War II with small displacement, single-cylinder machines. Designer Fabio Taglioni arrived in the 1950s, adding a shaft driven overhead cam and desmodromic valve actuation to Ducati's racing engines. By 1971, both these features were offered on some of the company's road-going models, and those single-cylinder Ducatis were potent machines.

Venturing into the sport-bike market in 1971, Ducati introduced a 750-cc V-twin with the traditional shaft-driven cams and desmodromic valve gear. It was followed by larger-displacement versions that met with great success, and quickly took over Ducati's line.

But there was a time when it appeared as though the Italian company, with its famous "desmo" powerplants, was on its last legs. Luckily for sport-bike enthusiasts, Cagiva entered the picture and rescued the Ducati name from the brink of disaster.

To develop the Montjuich, which was named for the famous Montjuich Park Gran Prix circuit in Barcelona, Spain, Cagiva management lured Fabio Taglioni out of retirement to breathe new life into the tired 90-degree V-twin. Having done so, Ducati assembled the rest of the motorcycle—sparing no expense—for racing homologation. Only 200 of the 750-cc bikes were built, a mere 10 finding their way to the United States.

1. The Montjuich was a serious racing bike, which meant no passengers, no air filters, and no turn signals.

2. Massive Brembo floating-ventilated disc brakes were found front and rear, and dry weight was a mere 367 lb.

①

1994 Buell S2 Thunderbolt

By combining the latest hardware from Buell with the financial backing of Harley-Davidson, the S2 Thunderbolt was poised to make a full-scale attack on the popular sport-bike market. Eric Buell was certainly no amateur when it came to performance motorcycles, as he had been designing and building Harley-powered sport-bikes since the late 1980s. In the past, however, production had rarely exceeded 100 to 120 units per year; with Harley-Davidson newly entrenched as a 49-percent partner, annual sales were expected to number in the thousands.

Harley-Davidson tried marketing its own sports-oriented motorcycle back in 1977 with little success, but that bike, the XLCR, could hardly match the performance of lighter, more powerful Japanese entries. The S2, boasting Buell's latest technical refinements, promised to be a stronger contender. Powering the S2 was a modified 1203-cc V-twin from the Harley-Davidson Sportster, which rested on rubber mounts to reduce vibration to a more comfortable level. Each of the space-age frames was built by hand from chromoly tubing. Out front was a huge 13-inch brake rotor gripped by a six-piston Brembo caliper, while in back, an aluminum swingarm activated an extension coil-over shock mounted beneath the engine.

The combination of a low center of gravity, sophisticated suspension, and compact 55-inch wheelbase ensured that the Buell S2 Thunderbolt handled like no other Harley-powered bike before it. And the Sportster-based engine ensured that it sounded like no other sport-bike on the road.

1. As did the Harley Sportster from which it garnered its engine, the S2 used a toothed belt to drive the rear wheel instead of a chain.

2. Note the black muffler that dumps its exhaust just ahead of the rear wheel (it's barely visible beneath the left side of the engine); most other sport-bikes display their mufflers prominently.

3. Headlight and taillight are flanked by decorative grilles.

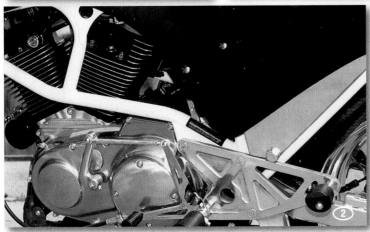

1994 Harley-Davidson FLHTC Electra-Glide

In motorcycle parlance, the Harley-Davidson FLHTC represents what's known as a "full dresser," being equipped with luxuries riders of 30 years ago never even envisioned.

It wasn't until the 1940s that windshields became common, the military being among the first to use them—with the hope of stopping more than just wind from going through the rider's hair. Later in the decade, Harley-Davidson offered a roll-up windshield as an option on civilian bikes.

In those days, riders felt lucky to get instruments and warning lights on their mounts. As might be expected, motorcycling has come a long way since then. The FLHTC Ultra Classic Electra-Glide features air-adjustable suspension, quiet belt-drive, an electronic cruise control, CB radio, AM/FM amplified stereo with weather band that includes remote controls for the passenger, a spacious rear trunk, and heavily-padded seats with backrests, all of which make its passengers feel right at home—even when they're miles away.

In the old days, riders probably never dreamed that touring could be so luxurious. Nowadays, they don't have to.

1. Eighty-cubic-inch Evolution V-twin introduced in 1984 provides sufficient power to motivate the dresser's 765 lb.

2. The back half of the seat is flanked by speakers for the stereo; they have their own volume control as well.

3. Script on the front fender says a mouthful. "Ultra Classic Electra-Glide"

4. There's storage space aplenty on the FLHTC, including compartments in the lower fairing.

1998 Triumph T595

Triumph made a resurgence in the 1990s, though it was admittedly in name only; the original company was long gone by that time, as was the fabled factory at Meridan.

Credited with the return was John Bloor, who had put up the money to fund a range of completely new motorcycles that was six years in the making. They were powered by water-cooled triples and fours displacing 750 to 1200 ccs, and included standard, sport, touring, and eventually dual-purpose models.

The most sporting of the new Triumphs were the 750-cc three-cylinder and 1000-cc four-cylinder Daytonas. Wrapped in sleek bodywork, they were powerful enough, but taller and heavier than their Japanese rivals. That all changed in 1997.

With the introduction of the T595 that year, Triumph was back in the game. This revised Daytona sported a 955-cc fuel-injected triple in a new alloy frame, and the combination proved potent. And though the Triumph name was perhaps more closely associated with "standard" models, the T595 quickly became the marque's bestseller.

1. Sleek bodywork of the T595 combined with a strong 955-cc, water-cooled, fuel-injected triple to produce a competitive sporting mount.

2. These new Triumphs had little association with the Triumphs of old, as about the only thing carried over was the stylized logo—and even that was changed some.

2002 Harley-Davidson V-Rod

While Harley-Davidson's traditional V-twins shared a 45-degree V, air cooling, and two valves per cylinder, all that went out the window when the VRSCA V-Rod was introduced for 2002.

Although the engine of the V-Rod was unlike any that had ever graced a Harley-Davidson showroom, it really wasn't anything new to the company itself. Back in the mid-1990s, Harley-Davidson had raced a VR1000 powered by a 60-degree V-twin with liquid-cooling, double-overhead cams, and four valves per cylinder. And low and behold, that's the same configuration adopted for the V-Rod.

Specs for the V-Rod's Revolution V-twin included 1131 ccs of displacement, electronic sequential-port fuel injection, and plug-top ignition coils. Though it was hardly large by Harley-Davidson standards, its claimed 115-horsepower output topped anything the company had ever offered to the public.

Yet the revolutionary V-twin was hardly the V-Rod's only departure from Harley-Davidson tradition. Long and low, it featured an exposed tube frame, anodized aluminum body panels, an ovoid-shaped headlight, and a steeper fork angle than any other bike in the company's lineup. Furthermore, only one other Harley-Davidson of the period boasted solid wheels front and rear, and those of the legendary Fat Boy were of a different design.

As might be expected, some Harley-Davidson traditionalists took umbrage at the revolutionary V-Rod. But its power and style have since made the company's first "performance custom" a legend in its own right.

1. The ovoid headlight featured on this bike is much different from the traditional Harley-Davidson headlights.

2. The instrument panels on Harleys have come a long way—from the simply attributed bikes of the early 20th century that featured just a speedometer to this 2002 model with a speedometer, odometer, tachometer, fuel gage, headlight and turn signal indicators, and temperature and oil pressure warning lights.

3. Reminiscent of Harley's seminal Fatboy series, the solid wheel set adds to the anodized-aluminum body's sleek look.

2008 BMW R 1200 GS

BMW's R 1200 GS is an unlikely mix of stalwart tradition and modern technology that some credit with starting the whole "travel-adventure bike" market.

Although BMW has offered numerous other types of powerplants since it began motorcycle production in the 1920s, the company is best known for its original horizontally opposed twins, updated versions of which continue to power many current BMW models.

It appears the R 1200 GS carries normal telescopic forks, but that's certainly not the case. Called "Telelever" forks, the lower legs are connected by a cross brace mounted above the fender, with the brace being suspended by an A-arm that hinges off the frame. The A-arm is controlled by a single coil-over shock, which on 2008 models could be optioned with electronic adjustment.

It's possible the GS's protruding proboscis has some aerodynamic benefit, but it likely isn't maximized toward that end. It flows right into the bodywork that tops the fuel tank, which in turns flows into the seat, the back half of which can be removed to accommodate cargo.

When first released back in the 1980s, BMW's GS models combined the features of a sport bike, an enduro bike, and a touring bike, overlapping their qualities like a vehicular Venn diagram. That has proven to be a wildly successful formula for BMW, one that inevitably spawned a number of competitors in the marketplace. But with its unique BMW mechanicals and avant-garde styling, it's pretty safe to say that none of them have come out quite like the R 1200 GS.

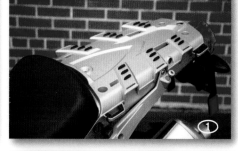

1. The back half of the seat can be removed to attach storage cases for touring.

2. Dual front disk brakes provide excellent control and traction while braking with the antilock brake system.

3. The single-sided swingarm allows for the back wheel to be removed more easily than the double-sided swingarm system.

4. Although the 2008 BMW R 1200 GS could be ordered from the factory with either spoke or cast wheels, those fitted to this example are special light-weight wheels used on the BMW HP2 Sport, a high-performance limited-production superbike of the same era.

2008 Kawasaki Z1000

One of Kawasaki's landmark motorcycles was the Z-1 900 of 1973. Bred to "one up" the venerable Honda 750 Four, it did just that with a double-overhead-cam inline four boasting 903 ccs of displacement and a claimed 82 horsepower. Later versions were called "KZ900," which was upsized for 1977 to become the KZ1000—a bike that became a legend in its own right (in no small part due to its long-time use by "CHIPS," the California Highway Patrol).

Fast forward to the New Millennium. For 2003, Kawasaki introduced the Z1000 as a "naked bike" (essentially a sportbike stripped of its full fairings) with a 953-cc, 16-valve, liquid-cooled transverse four. Some considered it the spiritual successor to the KZ1000; nearly all considered it a darned fine example of the naked-bike breed.

Originally painted pearl white and equipped with larger mufflers along with upper radiator fairings incorporating integrated turn signals, this particular 2008 Z1000 was altered to mimic the look of the original Z-1 of 1973. Most notable are its slim, "period" mufflers and orange and brown (some refer to it as "Root Beer") paint scheme that distinguished the Z-1, which—like the Z1000— also carried a small tail fairing. The engine of this example was dressed up with some chrome touches that likewise gave the otherwise all-black powerplant a closer resemblance to that of its inspirational predecessor.

With its more powerful engine being joined by modern inverted forks, single-shock rear suspension, and triple disc brakes, this "reimagined" Z1000 combines the look of the past with the performance of the present.

1. A throwback to the 1973 Z-1, this "Root Beer" paint job pays tribute to this modern bike's predecessors.

2. The Z1000 can be pushed to the brink with its 11,000-rpm redline.

2009 Buell 1125CR

After branching off to build his own motorcycles in the 1980s, former Harley-Davidson engineer Erik Buell came up with some innovative technologies that met with a roller-coaster of success.

Although his first effort was a racing motorcycle, Buell began building street bikes in 1987, the first being a series of sportbikes powered by Harley-Davidson's Sportster-based, racing-inspired XR1000 V-twin. Later models used variations of the production Sportster engine, some highly modified to produce more than 100 horsepower.

But the real innovations behind Buell's motorcycles had to do with the chassis. Early models carried the fuel inside the frame rails and the oil in the swingarm, and the "Zero Torsional Load" large-diameter front brake disc was mounted to the wheel rim rather than to the hub. The bikes were generally not as quick as those from Japanese and European rivals, but they handled very well, and the V-twin produced loads of low-end torque and a distinctive exhaust note.

In 1993, Harley-Davidson bought into Buell, and fully owned the company as a subsidiary by 2003. During this period, a flurry of Buell models were produced, ranging from sportbikes to sport-touring bikes to "adventure touring" bikes. There was also the Blast, a single-cylinder bike aimed at beginning riders.

In 2007, Buell moved away from using Sportster engines, choosing instead a much more advanced double-overhead-cam, 4-valve-per-cylinder, water-cooled, 72-degree, 1125-cc V-twin built by Rotax of Austria. Reported to produce 146 horsepower—far more than the Sportster-based engines—the Rotax went into a model called the 1125R, essentially a sportbike without a full fairing. A variation of this bike arrived for 2009 as the 1125CR, the "CR" signifying its "Café Racer" styling.

The 1125s turned out to be the final production Buells built under the Harley-Davidson umbrella. Although more than 130,000 Buells had been sold over the years, profits were not always impressive, and the parent company decided to concentrate its efforts on its traditional cruiser and touring bikes.

1. The 1125CR has some serious street power with 146 horsepower redlining at 10,500 rpm.

2. The "Zero Torsional Load" front disc brake can be seen mounted near the rim of the wheel as opposed to near the hub of the wheel.

2014 BMW S 1000 RR

Until recently, when people thought "BMW," this was probably not the bike they envisioned.

Throughout most of its history, BMW was best known for sturdy but relatively mundane motorcycles steeped in tradition and built with quality. But as the "superbike" craze took hold in the early 1970s—and grew ever stronger as the years went by—BMW began exhibiting some newfound muscle.

The first example was the performance-oriented R90S that arrived for 1974, among the first factory superbikes to sport front and tail fairings. In the late 1980s came the K1, a futuristic-looking sport-tourer boasting full bodywork, antilock brakes, and a longitudinally mounted 1000-cc water-cooled inline four laid on its side.

Fast forward to 2009. BMW decided to enter the Superbike World Championship series and designed a new bike just to do so: the S 1000 RR. Which soon after arrived in a street version.

Bucking every BMW tradition, the S 1000 RR was notable for . . . its conformity. Conformity to the established norm, that is. Most significant in this regard was its use of a transverse-mounted inline four with double-overhead cams, four valves per cylinder, and chain drive. Yes—exactly what most superbikes had long used.

Yet somehow (perhaps the exotic titanium valves had something to do with it), the S 1000 RR turned out to be a superbike hero. In racing trim it won a slew of events, including nine out of ten in the 2010 FIM Superstock 1000 Cup series, notable because the competition bikes closely resemble those in the showroom.

As specs for this 2014 version include a rated output of 193 horsepower at 13,000 rpm (with a 14,200-rpm redline!) and a road-ready weight—with a full tank of fuel—of only about 450 lb, it seems BMW has found some very strong muscles indeed.

2017 Harley-Davidson CVO Pro Street Breakout

In "The Old Days," if you wanted your motorcycle to stand out, you had to do the customizing yourself. That not only required a lot of work and expense, it often meant removing perfectly good parts that were sent to the corner of the garage to collect dust.

But what if you could just buy a customized bike right off the showroom floor . . . saving the work, some of the expense, and that precious garage space?

Harley-Davidson has been doing just that for nearly 20 years. Since its inception in 1999, The motor company's Custom Vehicle Operations (CVO) has produced a variety of limited-edition machines, typically picking just two to four models each year to get special treatment.

Arguably the most stunning of the 2017 crop was the CVO Pro Street Breakout. Riding the company's softail frame (which looks like the hardtail frames of yore, but has a separate rear section that pivots over bumps), it combined unique paint, wheels, bodywork, and steeply raked inverted forks with Harley-Davidson's 110-cubic-inch Twin Cam 110B engine to create a bike that screamed "custom" with a very strong V-twin voice. And its few lucky buyers didn't have to waste their weekends creating it.

A unique paint treatment, distinctive headlight fairing, lower-frame chin spoiler, and Screamin' Eagle air intake help give the Pro Street Breakout a custom look, despite the fact it came that way right from the factory.